W9-BQZ-611

A NEW START FOR THE CHILD
WITH READING PROBLEMS

A NEW START FOR THE CHILD WITH READING PROBLEMS

A Manual for Parents

Revised and Updated Edition

by

CARL H. DELACATO, ED. D

*Director, The Centre for
Neurological Rehabilitation
Morton, Pennsylvania*

David McKay Company, Inc.
New York

Library of Congress Cataloging in Publication Data

Delacato, Carl H
 A new start for the child with reading problems.

 1.   Reading—Remedial teaching.   I.   Title
LB1050.5.D45   1977   372.4'3   77-4228
ISBN 0-679-50760-4
ISBN 0-679-50765-5 pbk.

10 9 8 7 6 5 4 3 2 1

·MANUFACTURED IN THE UNITED STATES OF AMERICA

TO JANICE
AND OUR CHILDREN LIZ,
HANK, DAVID, AND NED

For their patience and understanding

CONTENTS

Photographs follow page 108

PREFACE

THIS IS A BOOK for the mothers and fathers of children who suffer from reading and learning problems. Being the parent of such a child is both frightening and frustrating. The increasing number of such children all around us is alarming, and the fact that so little is being done to help these youngsters only increases our fears that the children will forever be denied a solution to their problems.

Parents are bombarded with sad statistics of the millions of children who do not learn to read well enough to survive in our technological culture. Parents are told that such children will be deprived economically and socially. With so many reading problems among the young people of our nation, (even the Federal government has placed the numbers of reading failures in the millions), a new kind of solution *must* be found.

Schools have failed these children. Government programs have been unsuccessful in their efforts to help children with learning disabilities. As a result, the number of children with learning and reading problems continues to grow.

This book proposes a different solution for reading and learning problems. It explains my view that reading and learning problems are the result of faulty or inadequate development of the child's nervous system, *not* the result of faulty teaching methods or lack of motivation on the pupil's part.

Furthermore, this book teaches you *how* to solve your child's problem, at home. The early chapters give the background and theory of the Delacato technique. Following that, there are tests for you to administer to your child to ascertain where his neurological development is incomplete. The final chapters contain a step-by-step daily plan for solving your child's reading and learning problems at home.

The success of this home program can be measured in the overwhelmingly positive response from readers of the first edition of this book, first published in April 1970. We have received innumerable thank-you letters (almost daily for seven years!) from all parts of the world and as far away as Australia. The appreciative parents recount their successful results after following the Delacato technique. This book is also published in Dutch, German, Hebrew, and Italian.

Only through you, the parents, working with your own children at home, can we finally begin to solve the reading and learning problems surrounding us. After you have used this learning program with your child to complete the development of his central nervous system, you will discover that he is able to learn and to read at school no matter what teaching methods are used.

ACKNOWLEDGMENTS

NEW IDEAS and books are rarely the result of one man's work. The ideas expressed in this book are not exceptions. I am deeply grateful to the many people whose thoughtful contributions made this book possible.

This book recounts the story of how I arrived at a new approach to solving reading and learning problems. It tells of my introduction to the ideas of Temple Fay, M.D., the famed neurosurgeon, and of my early work at Chestnut Hill Academy, and of the founding of the Institutes for the Achievement of Human Potential.

In 1973, I left the Institutes in order to found The Centre for Neurological Rehabilitation with Robert J. Doman, M.D., my long-time co-worker. The Centre, located in Morton, Pennsylvania (a Philadelphia suburb), treats all types of brain-injured children and adults in addition to children with learning and reading problems. It also has a special division for autistic children. Other clinics under The Centre's direction are located in Barcelona, Spain, and La Habra, California.

This new approach to solving reading and learning problems has been advanced and improved through the constant dedication and hard work of the following senior staff members at The Centre: John F. Unruh, clinical director, and James F. McGonagle, director of therapy.

These techniques are being used and refined in the Delacato Clinics overseas that Janice Delacato, my wife, and I co-direct. I am deeply grateful to Professor Elsbeth Fend-Engelmann and Waltraud Hunze, supervisors of the Delacato Clinic in Cologne, West Germany. I also acknowledge my indebtedness to Augusto Paris, M.D., Nilo Fracassi, Elio Del Castello, and Santé Ventresca, supervisors of the Delacato Clinics in Avezzano and Sulmona, Italy.

My gratitude extends to Emmie Horowitz and Jennie Sasson, supervisors of the Delacato and Delacato Diagnosis and Treatment Project in the Federation of Kibbutz Movements in Israel. I also wish to acknowledge my appreciation to Beno Rothenberg, Pinhas Narkis, Ruth Ennis, and Tova Adiv, supervisors of the Delacato TIKVA Clinic in Haifa, Israel.

Most of all, I am grateful to Eugene B. Spitz, M.D., friend and co-worker, whose neurosurgical service and team provide constant diagnostic and medical help to the children. Gene Spitz, famed and courageous neurosurgical pioneer and innovator, supplies us with solutions to the seemingly unsolvable neurological problems. Through his ability to listen and willingness to teach, our techniques continue to evolve and to improve.

Because all these people are concerned about children and because they have the courage to try new approaches to old problems, this book has become a reality. I shall always be grateful for their help.

PART ONE

THE SEARCH FOR AN ANSWER

Chapter 1

JOINING THE MIRACLE MEN

FAY WAS A formal man. He wore a vest even on this warm October morning and I glimpsed his Phi Beta Kappa key as he reached out to shake hands. His handshake was firmer than it needed to be. I found later that strong hands are an occupational disease among neurosurgeons.

"Welcome to our group," he said.

So this was Fay, the famed and controversial Dr. Temple Fay, about whom I had read so much and about whom I had been taught, sometimes derisively, at the University of Pennsylvania. Although he was only 58, he was a legend in his own time. In my own thoughts I had always called him Fay, but in real life I was always to call him "Sir" or "Dr. Fay," as was everybody else who ever dealt with him.

He wiped his close-cropped mustache with his handkerchief, a constant habit, and took me over to the other side of the huge room filled with tables. "This is Dr. Robert Doman, another young man on the team. Dr. Doman is a physiatrist." I had never met a neurosurgeon before, and I had never met a physiatrist; furthermore, I didn't have the foggiest idea what a physiatrist was.

Robert Doman wore a white coat and was professorial in manner. He seemed to be about my age and was obviously trying to make me feel comfortable, but his quiet and assured man-

3

ner, coupled with his white coat, only helped to make me more ill at ease. He wore glasses, on the thick side, since he had had scarlet fever as a boy. I was to find out later that he was a highly trained and skilled physician, whose specialty was physical rehabilitation. Bob's reaction to my handshake was a friendly "There's a lot we can learn from you, Carl." I didn't know what he could possibly learn from me, or I from him, but it was reassuring.

Fay next took me over to a table where Glenn Doman was sitting, in shirtsleeves. He was resting, having just carried a child into the next room. I was here to do an I.Q. test on a child. I was sure that the child I was to test was in another part of the building. I hoped so.

"Hi, welcome aboard," smiled Glenn Doman, as he pumped my hand. I noticed that his head seemed a bit too large for his athletic body, and his hands too small. But he smiled and I was reassured.

The three of them escorted me into the next room. My fears were justified. The child I was to test was lying, face up, on a table. His distorted and twisted little body seemed in constant motion. He was deaf, couldn't talk, couldn't move, and his sunken, crossed eyes were searching every corner of the ceiling. His skinny legs were horribly twisted. He was frightening to behold.

Dr. Fay very formally introduced me to the sad-eyed parents and then dismissed them. He and the Domans stepped back and waited.

Nothing I had ever seen, heard, or read prepared me for this. To keep my heart from pounding too loudly, I walked around the child and peered at his pathetic body in open-mouthed astonishment. I had just met for the first time in my life four new creatures—a neurosurgeon, a physiatrist, a physical therapist, and a severely brain-injured child. I hoped it was the last time I would ever lay eyes on any of them. I vowed I'd never leave the warm comfort of my school again.

Chestnut Hill Academy, an ivy-covered boys' school, hidden in 30 acres of beautiful lawns and trees, was only two miles away. It seemed like a million miles. While driving the two tree-shaded miles I had thought about my future. I was the principal of the Junior School, I had a new Doctor's Degree from Ivy Leagued Penn and I had recently married a Bryn Mawr graduate —the three basic qualifications for becoming the headmaster of some plush, private school. It was 1952 and I had it made.

The only slight problem in my rosy, 28-year-old world was one question, "Why did some kids in my school not learn to read well, even though they were taught well and were bright and hard-working?" Perhaps doing some testing of different types of kids might help me to learn more.

"Dr. Delacato, what is your opinion as to his I.Q.?"

Fay's question jolted me out of my reverie. My degree was so new that anyone calling me "Doctor" jolted me, and now his terrible question. In utter defeat and resignation I looked at the three of them standing there so securely. I didn't like the brain-injured child because he frightened me and, furthermore, I didn't like the three of them. I looked down at the child and said, "It beats hell out of me."

I had started for the door, heading back on the road to that headmastership in the plush, private school, as Glenn Doman put his hand on my shoulder and, talking to Fay, said "Sir, I think we've found an honest one. Come on, Carl, let's all have a cup of coffee."

Somehow, his hand on my shoulder didn't seem so small.

It was probably the longest coffee break in history. Sitting at a small table in the kitchen in the Norwood Center, Fay handed me the reports of two other psychologists on the same child. "The I.Q.s are 10 and 18, both in the hopeless idiot range."

I was astounded! How could you test a child who couldn't move, hear, or talk, and who could barely breathe? How could they tell what his brain was like by looking at his distorted body?

How could they use I.Q. tests designed for normal children on this completely disabled and abnormal child? This poor kid's brain was locked up inside him; it was totally deprived. There was no channel into it. Anyone giving him an I.Q. score wasn't measuring his brain, but was measuring the barriers between the world and his brain, which the brain injury had created. I was shocked at the reports and said so.

Fay and the Domans smiled and handed me the reports to read again. This was my first lesson, one of many, about the brain.

They told me they were a rehabilitation team, which, they explained, meant they took care of brain-injured children and adults. Fay did the neurosurgery which was required, and then the three of them set up programs of activities to start the patient functioning again. "Most of the patients live here at the Center and work on the program each day," Glenn said.

I thought back to the child with the distorted body. Could they help that pathetic child? I was sure nothing could help him. But if these men could, they were truly miracle men. The morning passed quickly, as I listened.

In midafternoon Fay and Bob excused themselves to make hospital rounds. Glenn and I talked. I was comfortable with him; he was optimistic and enthusiastic. I told him about my interest in reading problems and the different approaches I had tried on reading problems during the past seven school years and summers. "No one seems to have a solution to reading problems." He didn't seem interested.

He listened politely, but he was more interested in my training as a psychologist. All discussion with Glenn ended with the brain—a subject which was new to me and not one of my main interests. I was interested in the mind, not the brain, and Glenn could sense it.

In order to entice me, he showed me models of the human brain; then he showed me a row of laboratory jars containing pieces of Dr. Fay's pathological specimens removed from the brains of patients. He grew excited as he told me in detail how he had watched Fay take this one out, or about the great result with this one.

Glenn went on and on about each of the brains in the jars. There was something exciting about holding a human brain in your hand, wondering what thoughts, aspirations, hopes, abilities it once represented. I found myself staring at the gray specimens with more interest.

"I see you could easily become as fascinated with the brain as I am, Carl. Without it there is nothing, no movement, no sounds, no speech, no vision—no mind. If you'd like to learn more about the brain, which is the basis of the mind—and see live, coral-colored, pulsating brains, instead of these dead gray ones—why don't you join us?"

There was more blood than I imagined there would be. That skinny kid couldn't lose much blood and live and, besides, I had never found the sight of blood pleasant. Fay was a masterful surgeon. Glenn and I stood there watching. I felt a little silly in a surgical gown and mask. During the years ahead, I was to find that I would never become totally at ease with the sight of the blood or with the surgical gown.

For six months I had been part of the team. These were exciting days, full of learning and full of terror. When you go into a new field surrounded by three compulsive teachers you are uncomfortable. They tried to teach me so much, helped me to do so many new things. New things are frightening when you don't feel up to them. Yesterday we had tested this child; today the brain surgery—and if he survived it, in a few weeks we would discover what changes in his behavior, capacity, mobility, and even personality were made by the operation. It was my early training in learning which part of the brain was for what function.

I felt a little guilty as I left school early each afternoon, to join the team. I was learning about the human brain and hoped it would help in solving my real problem—the reading problem. There were still too many wonderful, bright, and hard-working kids in my school who weren't learning to read as they should. Interestingly, if you read something to them, giving them information through their ears, they could understand, but when you gave them the same words to read or to absorb through the eyes, they failed. Reading problems seemed different from hearing or understanding problems, and yet, it was the same brain.

As a team, we saw hundreds of brain-injured children and adults during the first year. One was a well-known retired judge, brought to us because he had suffered a stroke, the result of a hemorrhage in the left side of his brain. He could not use the right side of his body, could not move his right arm or his right leg, and he had also lost the ability to talk. He could, however, carry out simple commands such as "blink your eyes" or "raise your left hand," so we knew he could understand us, at least to some degree.

As far back as 1865, Broca, a French physician, had pointed out that one-half the brain was the language half. The language half of the brain also controlled the side of the body on which one was *handed*. The hemorrhage had taken place in the judge's language hemisphere.

Our job was to help the judge learn to walk again. We stood him up, with Glenn on one side holding him up and me on the other. The judge was frightened, but not nearly as frightened as I was. His body was limp, and he was heavy. What if he slipped out of my hands and fell? Didn't Glenn know I was a schoolteacher and not a therapist? Each day I admired the judge's courage more. I hoped he couldn't sense how frightened I was each time I helped him to walk.

"Hold him up straight, Carl," Glenn would periodically whisper. He constantly praised the judge, saying with each attempted step, "Good work, Judge. Great." The judge reacted well and worked hard. As a result, in six months he had improved enough to walk alone, using a cane, and he had also somehow acquired the ability to speak a few words.

In light of his improvement we attempted to interest him in current events and reading for pleasure. If we succeeded, then at least he could enjoy his well-deserved retirement. We gave him newspapers to read, and books were left by his side at all times, but he looked at neither; he seemed to have some psychological block about them. He would not touch them or show any interest at all. We, and his family, exerted some pressure on him to read, but without success. During one of our discussions on the pleasure of reading, in fact, the judge broke into tears. He sobbed his secret to me in halting words: he could not read. As a result of the stroke, he could not even read his own name!

I was aware that he had lost considerable language ability, but since his speech had improved enough for him to carry on a rudimentary conversation, I had assumed that his reading had also improved. Although *he could understand quite a bit of what we read to him,* I found when I tested him that he could not read a single word.

Suddenly, it dawned on me that he was much like the reading-problem children, only more so. He could not read, yet he could understand the same material when it reached his brain through his ears. But he was not a child; he was an adult who, until the time of his stroke, had read avidly. The only difference was a ruptured blood vessel which had caused some injury to the left side of his brain. *Could it be that he had the very same condition as the children, only to a greater degree?*

About this same time a twelve-year-old boy, whom we shall call Steve, was brought to us for evaluation because he was having seizures in school. Steve had been attending a school for the mentally retarded for four years, where he received conscientious and expert reading instruction. Despite this, he could not read a single word. Neurological evaluation revealed a tumor in the child's brain. He was hospitalized, and the tumor was removed.

Two months after his discharge from the hospital, a very surprised school reported that he now was learning to read quite well. I questioned his teacher closely about possible changes in teaching methods, but there were none. Since the teaching technique had not changed, I could only conclude that something special in Steve's brain had been changed by the operation, increasing his ability to deal with words.

The judge had been a good reader all of his life; then an injury to the left side of his brain reduced him to a non-reader. Steve just couldn't learn to read; then after neurosurgery to remove a small tumor from his brain, he had become a reader.

A change in the structure of the brain changed reading ability. Harm to a brain through a burst blood vessel resulted in poor reading. Removing a tumor, which interfered with the brain's function, resulted in improved reading.

There might be a key to the reading-problem mystery in the brain. If there were an answer to be found in the brain, and if we could change the brain, we could change reading.

But who can change a brain or even influence a brain, short of drastic surgery?

Chapter 2

THE EYE AND THE BRAIN

It was snowing and dark when Glenn and his wife, Hazel, picked us up. We were going to the Fays' house for dinner. I sat in the front seat with Glenn. Our quiet conversation soon blossomed into a tirade about Fay. This had been one of his unreasonable days. Nothing we did was right. He made us feel that we didn't know at which end of the body the brain was to be found. He had been short-tempered, critical, and overly demanding. Glenn and I both agreed, "Look out, at dinner tonight!"

Hazel and my wife, Janice, sat quietly in the back seat.

The light splashing from the Fays' living-room windows onto Elbow Lane was warm and inviting. The snowflakes were growing larger; the snow would soon end. The girls smiled in anticipation, as I helped them out of the back seat.

"It looks so warm and Christmasy," whispered Janice as she passed me.

Somehow I felt cold and apprehensive. I didn't know whether Glenn was cold or not, but I knew he was apprehensive.

Fay and his charming wife met us at the door and we began a memorable evening, during which he was remarkably charming and gracious. He told our wives how bright and wonderful we were. His manner, although very courtly, was warm and paternal.

After dinner he led us into the living room to see some movies of his recent surgery. Hazel was a nurse, so I didn't worry about her and all the blood, but Janice was a schoolteacher, and I did worry about her. I was reassured when she leaned over to whisper, "Both you and Glenn look fat in those gowns." Following the films we went into the library, which contained some of the furniture owned by Mrs. Fay's great, great, great, great grandfather, J. B. Priestley, the discoverer of oxygen.

"Sit down here, gentlemen." As we sat in J. B. Priestley's chairs, he told our wives that this was a proper use of the chairs. These two young men had all the curiosity, drive, and ability personified by the famed Priestley.

I squirmed and glanced over at Glenn. I had never seen him so uncomfortable or embarrassed in my life. I would have laughed at him if I had dared.

Our wives were too silent in the back of the car, as we drove home. Then they started. How could we be so uncouth as to criticize that wonderful gentleman? We were terrible and ungrateful. If they had ever seen a gentleman, Dr. Fay was one. They were upset with both of us, and they never wanted to hear us criticize him again. He was the most charming man they had ever met, much more so than the two in the front seat!

Fay was an exceptional man. He could be charming or temperamental. He could be gracious or coldly critical. He could be witty or carping. He was always brilliant, however, and he was always preoccupied with the brain.

His preoccupation with the brain was catching. Each night I read about the brain until I fell asleep. In the morning I went to Chestnut Hill Academy, worked with my teachers and my reading problems. In the afternoons I was taught, even when I didn't want to be, at the Center. As we treated patients, the discussion was constantly about the brain. The months rolled by busily and happily.

Glenn and I became close friends, strangely enough, based on the fact that we had absolutely nothing in common except the brain. He was happy and outgoing, recently returned from the Army, where he had been one of the most decorated infantrymen in World War II. I was quiet and reserved, except when I was with Glenn. He had a strange effect on me, making me noisy and even quarrelsome. We were comfortable with each other, but the times we spent together were a constantly high-pitched talkathon. We were teaching each other everything we knew.

We spent as much time together as we could. Glenn was intrigued with what I knew about psychology because it was related to the brain, but he wasn't very interested in reading problems. The discussion centered on the brain or reading, depending on who had the floor. Glenn finally, in an attempt to quiet me on the subject of reading, asked what I had done about reading problems. "It can't be as hopeless as you picture it. Have you tried everything?"

I told him how, since 1945, I had experimented with the accepted approaches to the problem—psychiatry, psychology, tutoring, phonics and readiness—all of which resulted in failure.

The psychiatric approach had seemed to be a good place to start because it is true that children with reading problems do seem to have more than their share of emotional problems. A few upsetting questions arose, however. If poor reading was the result of psychological problems, why didn't the problem spill over into subjects which don't require reading? Many children who didn't read well did superbly with arithmetic. I had sent a number of children with reading problems to psychiatrists. Some time later, when they had completed their treatment, most of them returned not as good readers, but as happy, better-adjusted poor-readers. Later, while discussing this seeming lack of success with the psychiatrists, I was told that reading problems were not really the province of psychiatry, since psychiatry deals with personality problems which influence total school performance, not just reading. There seemed to be no solution to be found hidden in psychiatry.

I then began, methodically, to test the various theories in a summer school program. I had set up a six-week summer school program for twenty boys and girls, using new children and a new system each summer. We held our classes in my school and worked with children in the Philadelphia area. Since it might be possible that the way in which we taught reading might be causing emotional problems right in the class-room, I decided to test the psychological approach first.

We made reading fun! We gave the children interesting books and interesting lessons. They only used books written about their own special interests. We never scolded, instead we ladled out gobs of praise, and we insisted that their parents also be lavish with praise. There were daily therapy sessions, giving each child the opportunity to air his gripes about teachers, parents, reading, and school in general. The children enjoyed this part of the course and griped with gusto. The children made an average gain of slightly over one school year on our before-and-after tests. Follow-up testing a year later, however, indicated that, though we had improved them, almost all were still classified by their schools as reading problems. In short, although they had improved, we had not solved their reading difficulties. A new notion began to bother me: could emotional problems be the *result* of poor reading instead of the *cause* of poor reading?

The next summer I tried the phonetic, or alphabet approach. The constant cry during this period was "sound it out" or "what do the letters say?" But the results with the alphabet method were essentially the same as with the psychological approach. The average gain was about one school year—but a year later most of the children were still classified as reading problems by their schools. Again, although many had improved, I had not solved their problems. I kept one boy for two summers. He learned *all* the alphabet systems. During the second summer he was even pressed into action as a teacher of phonetics. He both learned and taught his phonetic lessons with marked ability. There was only one problem—he never learned to read.

The following summer I decided to try the tracing method. Under this method the child traced each word with his finger, while he said it and heard it. We tried to connect *feeling* the word with seeing it, saying it and hearing it. The results were the same—some growth, but the problem remained.

Next came the look-say method. The children were taught to memorize the words by sight. They made progress, the same as with other approaches, but a year later most were still reading problems at school. I tried combinations of all methods for two summers. The results were the same: some immediate progress but very few problems solved.

During the winters, I arranged to have a number of children tutored at school. They improved by repeating with a tutor the same work which had been covered in class. But the progress didn't last; the problem returned as soon as I stopped the tutoring.

Becoming more desperate, I looked at the theory of readiness, which states that the child needs more time to develop. The usual way of giving him more time is to have him repeat a grade or two. Taking some thirty children who had repeated and who seemed to have improved, I tested their reading. I found that they actually continued to be reading problems, but they did not stand out as much because the competition had been watered down. In effect, they still had reading problems but they were hidden by their less demanding school environment. Later, when students like these have had enough discouragement, they become "drop outs": recent statistics show that a great majority of drop outs had repeated one or more grades. In fact, dropping out has most of its beginnings in dropping back or repeating, and this occurs most often at the first-grade level.

The results of my experiments with each of these theories was some growth. But tragically, with all the effort, I had managed to *solve* the reading problems of only a few children—no matter which system was used, with the great majority I had failed.

Glenn listened to my account of failure without interruption. I could see that, for the first time, he could sense that the child with the reading problem was important. I told him the tragic statistics of our nation's reading problems.

It had been a good day. He had listened quietly and seemed impressed.

Without my knowing, Glenn told Fay and Bob about my search for a solution to reading problems. He presented a new idea.

"Would you allow Carl to see some reading problems here at the Center?" He had intrigued me with the brain and, happily, I had intrigued him with reading problems.

They agreed and now I could have my own small department and office, where I could see reading problems coming from all types of backgrounds and schools, in addition to my work with severely brain-injured children. But first they told me I had to look around to see if someone had the answer.

Perhaps my work with high I.Q.'d boys from Chestnut Hill Academy and my work during summers with children from Philadelphia wasn't varied enough. Perhaps someone, somewhere already had a solution to reading problems. If he did, we would find it and use it. Was there a single school or teacher with *no* reading problems? I visited two hundred school rooms, consisting of excellent schools and classrooms, mediocre schools and classrooms, and downright poor schools and classrooms. They all had good readers. Their average reading scores were slightly different, being higher in the better schools. Some schools in poverty-stricken areas had more reading problems than the usual twenty percent, but the one fact which was common to all the classrooms I saw was that they *all* had reading problems. *I did not find a single school devoid of reading problems.*

Even more disconcerting was the fact that the percentage of reading problems was virtually the same in all types of schools and in all types of classrooms. I returned to the Center without answers.

The constant search for the answer to an important problem made these exciting days. I had three jobs. My work at Chestnut

Hill Academy suffered. During the afternoons I worked with both brain-injured children and with reading problems at the Center. Periodically, a disturbing error occurred. I would be working with a mildly brain-injured child and would confuse him with one of the children with reading problems, or I would be working with a child with a reading problem and would find myself thinking of him as a mildly brain-injured child. I excused my confusion on the basis of having too many different jobs at one time.

We saw hundreds of children. They became a blur by the end of each day. It was late evening by the time we finished our work. Then we would sit and review the day's cases over coffee and a sandwich. I often suspected that these review sessions were so long because no one could muster the energy to go home.

Many interesting and helpful incidents occurred during this period. I occasionally saw a youngster who had previously never had a reading problem, but who had suddenly and mysteriously developed one. When I tracked such cases back to the onset of the problem, I found a fairly common set of circumstances.

One boy named Ted, for instance, had read well all of his school life, but in the middle of the fifth grade began to read poorly and to reverse words. He read "was" for "saw," or "on" for "no." In probing for causes I found that a month before Ted developed his reading problem he had fallen down, while skating, and had broken his right arm. With the right arm in a cast, he used his *left* hand for writing and eating, as best he could. His reading began to deteriorate, and the more he used his *left* hand, the worse his reading became. When the cast was removed, he went back to using his right hand and his reading began to improve spontaneously. Using what we had previously learned about the relationship of the brain to language, we analyzed what had taken place.

Ted had been completely *right-sided* prior to the accident, that is, he used the right side of his body as the skilled side. He wrote with his right hand and kicked with his right foot.

This meant that the *left* hemisphere of his brain was the language hemisphere, in which the storage of language took place. With a broken right arm, Ted began to use his left hand for writing and other things, such as eating and throwing. Thus, his hand use, at this point, was being controlled from the right, or non-language hemisphere and some sort of inefficiency was set up between the two hemispheres; some sort of inefficiency was taking place in the storing or recall of the language code. The result was a general slowdown in his reading and the appearance of reversals in reading.

When the cast was removed and Ted could use his right hand again, the brain hemisphere conflict seemed to be reduced and the reversals disappeared. Changing hand usage had influenced the way in which the brain operated, which in turn had influenced reading.

I saw another case, Jimmy, whose broken arm brought about a cure of a reading problem. This child had always had a problem; he reversed in his reading, and his spelling was hopeless. Then he fell and broke his arm. It was placed in a cast. A month later his parents noticed a rapid improvement in both reading and spelling.

Here again a change of hand use had influenced reading. I had already learned that a direct change in the brain, through neurosurgery or injury, could influence reading. Was it possible that a deliberate change in hand use, from right to left or vice versa, could change the brain without surgery?

The brain, it was well known, was split into two hemispheres —language and non-language hemispheres—and the language hemisphere controlled the skilled side of the body; that is, a person with the *left* hemisphere as the language hemisphere would be *right-sided*. If he damaged his left, or language hemisphere, he could no longer speak nor could he use the right side of his body, which was formerly his skilled side. The opposite, of course, was true with left-handers.

But what had not been guessed was the reverse of this situation: a change in hand use, from right-handedness to left, or from left-handedness to right, *might affect the brain*. This was not an entirely new idea in other fields. One school of thought in anthropology, for instance, feels that the changes caused in the development of the brain of early man, through the use of tools, was the significant factor in evolution. They stated that the "tool changes the tool user." In the field of rehabilitation this was a new and was to become a very provocative idea.

Even more provocative was what Jack was to teach me. He was totally right-sided and had been a good student all of his life. On a fishing trip he found some discarded blasting caps. He hit one of them and it exploded. His right eye was blinded by the blast. Although his left eye remained completely normal, his school work and reading soon began to deteriorate rapidly. His reading became painfully slow and he began to reverse letters in his spelling. Injury to Jack's right eye resulted in his becoming a poor reader.

Tony came to us as a reading problem, a prospective student for the summer course. Testing him, I found that he read at a 7th grade level, although he was going into the 9th grade. We found that he was right-handed but that he used his left eye for things like sighting or looking into a tube or microscope. Before summer school started, Tony's parents allowed him to go to an amusement park one afternoon for a last fling. He spent some time on a target range. Unhappily, one of the bullets exploded and a small piece of lead lodged in his left eye and festered. This was so painful that he was not allowed outdoors and, above all, he was not allowed to read or study at all during the summer. The infection finally was overcome, but the loss of a significant amount of vision in the left eye was permanent.

At the end of the summer we re-tested Tony's reading. He made a grade level test score of 10th grade. This represented a three years' growth in reading—much more growth than any of the students in our summer school had made during the same period of time! He had had no reading practice, no instruction.

The only thing that was different was that he could no longer see out of his *left eye,* and was now completely *right-sided.*

I had seen one boy who became a reading problem because of an accident, but happily Ted, Jimmy and Tony no longer had reading problems. They were successes. There was one disconcerting fact, however; I had had absolutely *nothing* to do with their success.

I had learned that changes in the physical structure of the brain changed reading. It was known that one side of the brain controlled language and that the same side controlled handedness and sidedness. If that side of the brain were damaged, then both language ability and skilled hand use were lost. We had, however, also seen instances where *changes in sidedness,* both with handedness and eyedness, influenced reading performance. If the use of the hands were one of the factors that decided which hemisphere of the brain became the language hemisphere, then we had at last found a way to get *inside the skull.* There *was* a way to change the brain, short of surgery.

Our reading problems all seemed to be reducible to some problem of vision, of an eye-brain relationship, and therefore I was spending a great deal of time learning all I could about vision and the brain.

We labored over numerous textbooks of neuroanatomy and neurophysiology. From our studies, it became increasingly evident that one could not deal with just one isolated sensation, i.e., vision, when dealing with a problem as complex as the inability to read and that the brain is dependent upon all areas for its integrative function. For the reader with a more technical interest, this is what we learned.

We know that man's brain differs from that of animals in having a thick outer mantle of cortex containing billions of cells which is called the neocortex. This cortex is divided into the left and the right side or hemisphere (as I have already described). The anatomist and physiologist had divided each hemisphere into four main lobes which seemed responsible for certain functions: *frontal* (motor function and emotion); *parietal* (sensation); *temporal* (hearing); and *occipital* (vision). See Diagram A. Each half of the cortex or hemisphere is divided by a large sulcus or valley called the *central sulcus*. In a general way, this central sulcus divides the brain into a posterior or back receptive or sensory portion and an anterior, or forward, portion that is related more closely to motor function. In the posterior part are located all the primary receptive areas, which receive specific sensory impulses from the lower centers of the central nervous system. The stimuli entering these primary areas produce sensations of a sharply defined character, such as distinct vision and hearing, sharply localized touch and accurate sensation of position and movement. However, these sensations at these primary areas do not attain the perceptual level necessary for the recognition of an object. This requires the integration of primary stimuli into progressively more complex neural relationships.

One of the most striking features of the human brain is its elaborate neural mechanisms for the more complex correlation and discrimination of sensory impulses and the greater utilization of previous experience. Therefore, even though major functions can be assigned to these lobes, of greater importance when studying function is the vast intricate network of interconnecting fibers which connect not only these lobes with one another but also small areas within these lobes to which scientists have assigned identifying numbers (see Diagrams A and B). The left and right hemispheres, on either side of the calcarine fissure, are also connected and interrelated by fibers. This then allows mutual exchange of incoming impulses with stored information which, when integrated and processed through the brain's intricate computer (made up of these association areas), produces interpretation of information from the environment, thought, and eventually response.

The effect of these areas on brain function has been studied

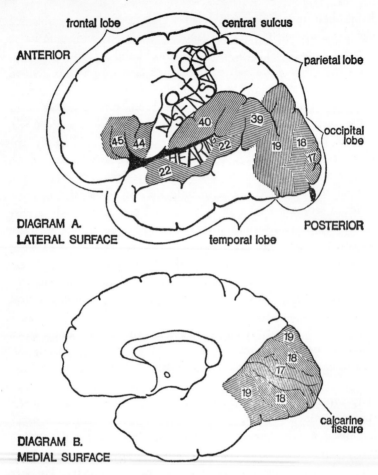

DIAGRAM A.
LATERAL SURFACE

DIAGRAM B.
MEDIAL SURFACE

by neurologists in patients in whom certain areas have been destroyed by disease, injury, or vascular occlusion. In the frontal lobe, areas 44 and 45, called Broca's area, when destroyed in the dominant hemisphere produced a loss of articulate speech. This is termed expressive aphasia. With this type of loss, the patient may be unable to speak or may say only one word over and over again or may manifest the loss by mispronouncing familiar words.

In the parietal lobe, area 39, or angular gyrus, seems responsible for certain language comprehension. Damage in this area in the dominant hemisphere produces dysfunction in the comprehension of written or printed speech which appears as an inability to recognize a written word, alexia—inability to read, and agraphia—inability to copy. Area 40 in the parietal lobe, also termed the supramarginal gyrus, when destroyed in the dominant hemisphere produces profound defects in the ability to understand or to express one's self by the symbolism that is called language.

The temporal lobe, where the primary centers for hearing may be found, also contains the associative acoustic area 22. Lesions in the dominant hemisphere of this area produce an auditory receptive aphasia or word deafness. The patient can hear what is said but cannot interpret the sounds, so that spoken language becomes difficult to understand or even completely meaningless.

The complexity of these mechanisms is nowhere more fully demonstrated than in the visual system. When light waves enter the eye, they pass through the cornea (which regulates the amount of light entering); lens (which focuses the light on the retina), and when they strike the retina they are converted into electro-chemical impulses. See Diagram C. If you look at a retina under the microscope, you see two kinds of structures—rods and cones. The cones are centrally located in an area called the fovea or macula. This area deals with precision vision, such as that required in reading, and with the identification of color. The rods are spread out through the remainder of the retina and they deal with varying shades of gray and with the detection of movement. As the retina changes the light wave energy into electro-chemical energy, the impulses then pass through the *optic nerve* to the *optic chiasm* which lies at the base of the brain. Here, many of the fibers split and cross over so that the right side of each retina sends information to the right side of the brain and the left side of the retina sends messages to the left side of the brain (see Diagram C).

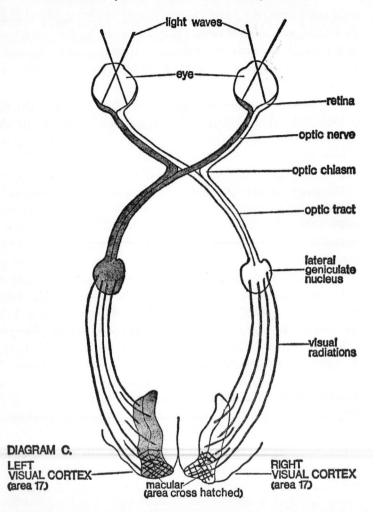

DIAGRAM C.

LEFT
VISUAL CORTEX
(area 17)

macular
(area cross hatched)

RIGHT
VISUAL CORTEX
(area 17)

The nerve fibers coming from the macula, where reading and color vision are centered, appear to pass through to the brain in a different pattern. This results in "macular sparing" when there is injury to the brain. It is probably the result of a difference in the splitting of the rod and cone fibers.

The nerve fibers then carrying the impulses by way of the

optic tract from the optic chiasm pass to the structure termed the *lateral geniculate nucleus*. From here the impulses are passed back through the brain by means of the visual radiations. Having passed through the brain via these visual radiations and maintaining a very strict definite arrangement relative to the retinal portion they represented, they terminate on the portion of the brain called the visual cortex (area 17 in Diagrams A, B, and C).

This is a very narrow strip of brain lying on each side of a sulcus called the *calcarine fissure* (Diagram B). Here, the electro-chemical changes that light has brought about in the retina are converted into the sensation of conscious vision but not into interpretive vision. However, the connections of the visual cortex to other areas of the brain become a very important part of the total concept of vision. Area 17 is integrated by association and connecting fibers to areas 18 and 19 of the same and opposite hemisphere. And it is also integrated with almost all other areas of the brain by connecting fibers which receive and others that send impulses.

Area 18 in association with area 19 provides following eye-movements and fixation of the eyes. Area 18 in association with area 17 is most important in interpretive vision function. If area 17 is destroyed, blindness will result, but if area 18 is destroyed, the patient will lose the meaning of vision. A person with such a lesion will walk around a ladder, indicating he sees it, but will be unable to name it and does not know how to use it. The associations built up in area 18 then make meaningful the objects seen with area 17 and its loss is termed visual agnosia.

Our textbook studies therefore had given us a better understanding and respect for the complexity of brain function and its vast network of interconnecting and interdependent areas as related to speech, language, vision, and more particularly, reading. However, even with this better understanding we still found no clear-cut answer to the ever-present question, "Why can't Johnnie read?"

Chapter 3

WARFARE ON READING

"GENTLEMEN, YOU have worked hard and you have learned well. Now, you are ready to talk to the world. I have an assignment for you." He was always formal, but this was unusual. Bob, Glenn, and I glanced at each other. Fay had never made such a statement.

"I want the three of you to go to New York next month to make this speech."

He handed us the invitation. Each of us was ecstatic but we didn't dare show it. The Institute of Physical Medicine & Rehabilitation was the largest and most prestigious rehabilitation institute in the world. Fay had enough faith in what we knew to allow us to represent him there to lecture on reflex therapy in the upper-motor neuron lesion.

"I'll be away for the week-end, you had better start working on your presentation. Good luck," and he was gone.

We were all delighted. It was a moment of great personal triumph for me, after only such a short time with the team.

We began to prepare our presentation the next morning. Fay had taught us that the human brain was a product of evolution. It evolved through the fish, amphibian, reptile, and mammal stages. Each new stage added a new layer to the old brain, right up to the human cortex or the large outer layer of man's brain, so man carries around with him all the older or lower levels of brains as spare parts, but doesn't use them. If, however, the newest or human portion of the brain is hurt, why not try to use the older layer of the brain?

If a man were brain-injured and couldn't walk, perhaps he could use a lower level of brain and creep instead. If he couldn't creep, Fay proposed that we pattern him. That is, the four of us take his head, arms and legs and move them through the motions of creeping. Perhaps through this patterning we could stimulate the older, more primitive, but undamaged, part of the brain into activity. Fay felt that the more ancient portions of the brain comprised man's reflexes and when we stimulated these old layers of the brain we were stimulating ancient reflex patterns. Based on these ideas our treatment theory was that we should treat the brain and not just arms and legs.

Glenn, Bob, and I wondered if he really wanted us to say the whole thing. We knew that accepted therapy for the brain-injured at that time was to massage and passively move the affected limbs. Fay had been criticized for his evolutionary views of the brain and for his patterning theory. Should we announce that through the patterning of these ancient reflexes, in the forms of complete movements, like crawling or creeping, the older layers of the brain could be stimulated to activity? Did we dare say this?

After days of discussion we decided to take Fay literally. Didn't he say we were ready to talk to the world? We wrote the speech, carefully discussing each word. Since we had no secretary, we asked one of the patients to type it when it was ready for the final reading. We took turns reading one paragraph at a time. It was Glenn's turn to read the last two sentences:

"It must then be considered as a basic principle that, when a lesion exists within the confines of the brain, treatment to be successful must be directed to the brain, wherein lies the cause, rather than to that portion of the periphery where the symptoms are reflected. Whether the symptoms exist in an almost indetectable subtlety in human communication or in an overwhelming paralysis, this principle must not be violated by those who seek success with the brain-injured patient."

There was a long silence. If the statement was so shocking to us, what in heaven's name would happen in New York next week? Even more important, what would happen when Fay heard it?

He listened very quietly a few days later, when we read it to him, nodding quiet approval throughout. He heard the last two sentences and said, "You've said in those few pages what I have been trying to say all my life. Perhaps the world needed to wait until 1953 to be ready to listen. Congratulations, you have said it well; in fact, much better than I have said it. I hope the world will listen."

Our speech went well. The Pennsylvania Railroad tracks from New York to Philadelphia were never smoother. We had been a great success, at least in our own minds. We could report this success to Fay, and now we could begin to talk to the world, a delightful world. Little did we know on that train ride that a new team had been born and that the world would not always be so pleasant.

The months went by busily. Our successes grew, and we began to receive invitations to speak at other institutions. We even received requests from therapists, doctors, and teachers to visit us to see our team in action. Some day we hoped that we might even have an Institution of our own.

My work spread into helping with the physical and speech rehabilitation of the patients. Bob and Glenn were becoming more interested in my reading problems. Bob examined them physically and Glenn checked their coordination.

I took them to Chestnut Hill Academy to see how children do learn to read. They enjoyed visiting the classrooms and watching my teachers in action. They agreed that it was one of the finest schools they had ever seen and I was pleased.

The first-grade children fell into a pattern year in and year out. Each year about forty percent of them learned to read by sight, that is, by the look-say method or the word-sight method; the teacher told the children the words and they remembered them. While working at remembering the words, they somehow developed their own secret system for breaking down and recognizing new words. Generally, these children became and remained the best readers and the best students.

The next forty percent of our six-year-olds generally had to be taught some analytic approach to reading—they just couldn't seem to learn to read by sight or through memory alone; they needed other cues. To this group we gave contextual cues, such as pictures on the page which told them what the reading was all about. We also arranged the sentences in their reading books so that the meaning helped the child to recognize new words. For instance, if we had a picture of a child looking at a hippopotamus and right under it a sentence, "Ted sees the hippopotamus," both the picture and the sentence helped the child to recognize the word "hippopotamus."

We also gave them structural cues, that is, the words are made so different from each other that they are more easily recognized. For example, the word "climb" is an easily recognized word structurally, because of its outline, as contrasted with the word "come." The outlines of the two words are quite different— climb come . Some children used these differences in outline to help remember words. This group also had to be taught to analyze the words alphabetically, if they were to learn to read. This group did learn to read but needed much more instruction and more analytical cues to recognize words. We found this group read slowly, word by word, at the secondary school level and, as a result, these youngsters never became excellent readers. Although this group never gained the high level of speed and proficiency in reading obtained by the group which learned by sight, these children were not considered reading problems. They became average readers.

The remaining twenty percent of the class were the reading

problems. They were taught by *all* methods. Most of the teachers' time, effort, and worry were spent on this group, but these children rarely learned to read well.

There was always one nagging fact present with this group. I knew that they were different because we couldn't teach them to read. I also knew that they weren't stupid because they learned other things very well. Why couldn't we teach them to read? These were the children we were failing, these were the children who so desperately needed our help. This failing twenty percent was studied long and diligently, but I could not find any difference between them as a group and our good readers as a group. I could not discover the cause of the problem.

During the summers I ran the reading clinic trying new approaches. Now, in addition to the regular teachers, I had Bob and Glenn who helped me to test the children.

All of our activities seemed to steal time and space. We now had a waiting list of children and adults, ranging all the way from severely brain-injured to those with reading problems. We needed more time, more space. We needed an Institution of our own.

The summer of 1955 was the best of all summers. We moved into our own Institution, in a palatial mansion on seven beautiful acres in Chestnut Hill and we called it the Rehabilitation Center at Philadelphia. It had been made possible for us by the family of a grateful patient.

Turning a sixty-room mansion into an Institution housing brain-injured children and adults requires a great deal of money or, in the event you don't have money, a great variety of skills. Because we had no money we relied on the latter. The summer of 1955 was the summer of painting, floor-tiling, carpentry, wall building, rug-laying, and treating patients.

Glenn was the Director, I was the Associate Director, Bob was the Medical Director, and Fay was the Neurosurgical Consultant. This administration was very efficient. For example, it settled the matter of salaries and solved the early budget problems quite well. Since Bob and Fay saw patients at the hospital, we decided that they would not receive any salary from the new Institution; since I received a salary from Chestnut Hill Academy, I did not receive a salary from the new Institution. Glenn sold his house and also borrowed some money. It all came to $40,000 which he gave to the Center. We paid him a salary which was just enough to cover the monthly payments for his indebtedness. Other problems were not so easily solved, and there were so many of them.

Staff had to be found, staff had to be trained, money to be found, patients to be treated, families to be seen, reports to be written; we were all working a seven-day week and it wasn't enough. Only during rare spare moments could we discuss any new findings or research with each other. Fay gradually, almost imperceptibly, began to relinquish his leadership role in our discussions.

Fay quietly let us try our own wings more and more. He gradually cut down the time he spent at the Rehabilitation Center. We knew, however, that he watched us closely from a distance. He took on more work as a government consultant, more lectures throughout the world and continued his writing. In his lifetime he wrote prodigiously and published 101 scientific articles.

Another important event occurred in 1955 which was to affect my life. It was the publication by Rudolph Flesch of the bombshell, *Why Johnny Can't Read*. The time was right for an explosion.

Up to this time reading problems had been the private province of the educator.

The buildup to this explosion started back in the nineteen-thirties, the free-wheeling days of the "Dewey Progressives," when educators held that children who didn't learn to read weren't necessarily stupid. The progressives boldly claimed that education up to that time had been woefully inadequate and pointed out that there were a large number of normally intelligent children who were not learning to read under the then accepted teaching system. The most shocking statistic they provided was that one out of three first-graders failed and had to repeat the first grade because they could not meet the second-grade reading standards. The progressives complained about the "rigidity" of the educational system and suggested many ways of liberalizing it. They promised better readers in the process. The progressive period ushered in the hey-day of the *word-sight* or *look-say* method of teaching reading. This system was the result of the "Gestalt" psychology movement, which proposed that one learns better by wholes instead of parts, wholes having more meaning than do parts. The Gestalt, or look-say, people held on well through the forties, but a rumble of dissatisfaction could be heard in the parents' ranks: the parents of the troublesome twenty percent who weren't learning to read.

Experiences during World War II threw a new light on the problem. A great many of the draftees could not read well. As soon as the war was over, military leaders complained about the weaknesses of our educational system. Something should be done, they insisted, about the disgraceful school situation. After the war, educators continued with the word-sight, or whole word method, but a few suggested that a more phonetic system might help. The phonetic is an older system, based on the alphabet and the sound components built from the alphabet. Under the phonetic system, children are taught to analyze words into the alphabetical components through knowing the sounds of the letters.

This postwar trend toward the old phonetic method caused an interested reaction, and some educators tried to stir up the educational community by suggesting that a greater use of it might be in order. Parents were not aware of the intramural conflict which resulted. There was a gead deal of comparing of the two systems at teachers' conferences during this period. The postwar baby boom and the G.I. Bill brought the problem into sharper focus. Now there were not only many more people, but many more people felt it necessary to have their children go on to higher education, and colleges were forced to pick and choose from the many applicants. For the first time they began seriously to use tests, and during the forties the College Board Examinations became a national institution.

Reading problems continued to plague the educators during the early fifties. Parents began to ask more questions about reading and P.T.A. meetings gradually evolved into debating societies. This growing concern was typified by one mother, who stated plaintively: "Here he is having trouble with second-grade reading. How can we think of college? I read that colleges take only the children out of the top half of their classes, and that twenty-five percent of all those accepted for college drop out. At this rate, my son doesn't have a prayer of getting into college, let alone graduating, if he does get in. And he is only eight years old!" Another ominous sign appearing at this time was the increased use of the term "drop out." It indicated that students who left school were becoming numerous enough to be labeled as a group, and the term became a source of disturbance for thousands of parents whose children found school a struggle.

As a result of all this emotional buildup during the early fifties, the very word "reading" became controversial, even when it was not followed by the word "problem." A spark at this time would set off explosions in every town across the country, and in 1955 it came.

Why Johnny Can't Read was on the best seller list for thirty weeks. The time was right. The various camps of parents and teachers were waiting for a spokesman, one whom they could follow enthusiastically or one whom they could oppose. Flesch took the position which was most popular with parents and least popular with teachers, and there are many more parents than teachers. He ignored the usual academic channels and wrote directly to the public; as a result, the teaching of reading, which had been for so many years the almost private province of the educator, now became a public issue.

Flesch stated flatly that there were too many children with reading problems and that they were the result of poor teaching, a statement which did not endear him to the teachers. It did endear him, however, to the many parents who agreed with him. He called for a return to the good old days of phonics as the antidote for the increasing number of reading problems. He told the public that children could not deal with whole words in learning to read. Since they could not deal with whole words, Flesch contended that reading should be taught by breaking up whole words into the letters, or the sound components of words.

Open warfare was the result of Flesch's book. Educators could not forgive him for taking his case directly to the public instead of going through academic channels. A large segment of the unsatisfied public saw an opportunity to pounce on education and did so with a vengeance. Organizations were formed across the country to implement the phonetic method of teaching reading. Movements such as "Back to Basic Education" and "Parents Reading Associations" were formed. Parent groups became openly vocal, insisting on a return to a phonetic approach. They exerted considerable pressure on their school systems, especially through P.T.A. meetings and, as a result, most schools moved toward a more phonetic approach to reading. Textbooks using a phonetic approach became educational best sellers, but the educational waters remained troubled.

Educators gave some token resistance at the outset but, sensing the pressure build-up of public opinion, they either gave in or went underground. Some few educators went so far as to agree with Flesch, but they did not do it very loudly, at first. Parent groups, heartened by their success, became even more vocal. Local newspapers took up the hue and cry. Young mothers became quite knowledgeable in whichever reading system they advocated, but only the maverick parent was in favor of the look-say method during the middle fifties.

Even as the smoke began to clear over the educational battle-ground, a stark reality appeared. The percentages of reading problems remained the same.

Reading problems were now a public issue. Suddenly, my world of research, full of logic and reason, became part of a national battleground. Parents would not be put off, they wanted answers to this new problem.

Because of one book, I was no longer dealing with a quiet, scientific search. Because of one book, I was now smack in the middle of a new public turmoil.

Chapter 4

THE LANGUAGE HEMISPHERE

HE WAS a giant. His thick neck, his heavy arms, his swarthy skin, his black eyes alternating between being too dry with intensity and too moist with sadness and his total inability to speak one word of English, made our first physician student quite a challenge.

He had come to us because his only son had broken his neck diving into the Bay of Rio de Janeiro and was now completely paralyzed from his neck down. Even though our new student was a renowned eye surgeon in his native Brazil, he was going to spend a year with us studying our techniques and watching us treat his teen-aged son. He worked hard, doing all kinds of jobs, many of them menial; his eyes were always on us, trying both to fathom our language and to understand our ideas.

We could not have guessed that our first student, Dr. Raymundo Veras, whose name means Truth in his native Portuguese, was to have such a profound effect on our ideas and our lives. Within four years those powerful arms were to lift me out of a steaming piranha-and-crocodile-infested river in the central jungle of Brazil so that my testing equipment wouldn't be ruined.

As time went by he learned a few English words and we a few Portuguese words, but our communication always seemed far better than our ability with language, especially when our opinions differed. As his son made progress, Veras's face and eyes became less clouded with sadness. He even laughed occasionally, a deep belly-laugh, which turned the entire Center into turmoil because it was so contagious. Everybody on the staff and all the patients had fallen in love with this improbable man.

It was disconcerting to be lecturing to an eye surgeon about vision, but it was helpful to have him around when I had questions. Whenever we talked about vision, Veras got that intense look. He would usually answer my questions by first smiling, then shaking his head, usually in disbelief of my question, and then draw a picture to explain his point.

Veras had been trained as an ophthalmologist in Brazil. His textbooks had been European, most of his teachers trained in Europe. There was a great emphasis on neuro-ophthalmology, or the study of the eye-brain relationship. His ideas on vision were in many ways different from ours. As we worked at a problem, he would begin to shout his newly learned American word—"No—No—No." It was difficult to work with Veras, he even disagreed with the textbooks which I showed him as proof of my arguments.

Bob finally intervened. "Carl and Raymundo, stop arguing. The truth of the matter is that we, in the States, look at perception differently from the people in Europe. Why don't you take what is best from the two points of view? There is no right or wrong, there is knowledge and dogma. You are both dealing in dogma—please deal with what is best from each and do it quietly."

I'm sure Veras didn't understand all the words but he understood Bob's message. He broke into his deep belly laugh. He looked like a swarthy and slightly mad Buddha as he guffawed.

My children with reading problems could certainly *see* the words on the page; however, they didn't get the meaning from them. What happens to the visual message when it gets to the brain was the next obvious step to work on. We carried out many experiments. Our experiments were concerned with the

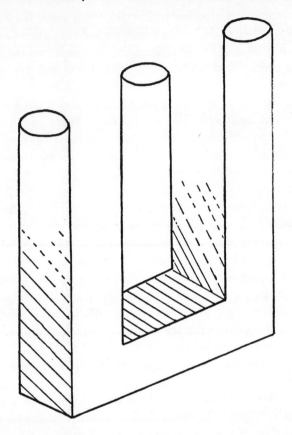

brain's main function, which is to interpret the incoming message. Its goal is to make sense out of the impulses or sensations which it receives. First it sets up a theory about each set of sensations, then checks it. If the pattern of the impulses fits the theory, it is accepted; if it doesn't the brain either changes the theory or tries to change or reject the sensations coming into it. When the brain is satisfied that its theory of what is coming in is correct, it accepts or perceives the information. But if the patterns of sensation coming to it are uncertain or ambiguous, the brain keeps searching and changing its decision. A good example of this is what happens when the brain is presented with an optical illusion. Try this experiment.

The picture opposite is a constant pattern of black with white lines; it is an unchanging stimulus. As the sensations from it arrive at your brain, a hypothesis is set up: "There are three legs extending from the main bar and it is a flat picture." When your brain attempts to check that theory, it is fooled, for what it sees is a U-shaped bar with two legs drawn in three dimensions. This is upsetting to your brain. Look at the picture for a minute; you will see it change back and forth from one hypothesis to the other, and all the time you know that the picture can't change because it is a printed unchanging combination of black with white lines. Because the picture is unclear and ambiguous, your brain is uncertain and keeps changing its decision.

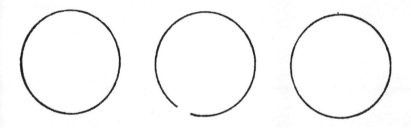

On the other hand, when the sensations come in as something which is *almost* understandable, your brain will change what it actually sees to what it wants to see, in order to make it completely acceptable. Look at the circles quickly a few times and you will find that often your brain chooses to ignore the fact that one is not a complete circle, and you will see it as a complete circle.

Look at the following page: You will notice that the dots shift from appearing to be separate dots to rows of dots, to columns of dots, to squares made by dots, all happening as you look at an obviously unchanging array of dots. Your brain keeps changing its mind as to what it is perceiving.

The brain has a natural tendency to try to make good sense out of the sensations that it receives.

When we blink our eyes no sensation enters the brain for a split second and for that split second the brain should register darkness. Our constant necessity to blink our eyelids to keep the eyeball clean and moist would, as a result, be constantly interrupting our activities if it were not for the brain's ability to ignore this momentary darkness which happens a number of times each minute all day long. As a result, we are never aware of these periods of darkness. They do not make good sense to the brain, so they are ignored and, as a result, our seeing seems continuous, although it is not.

Another example of the brain's very good sense is its ability to overlook the blind spot that exists in each eye. There is a spot in the retina, slightly toward the outside of the center point of vision in each eye, where the nerve fibers from the retinal receptors go through the retina on their journey into the brain. This spot is blind and there is such a spot for both eyes. But the brain ignores these blind spots, fills them in, so to speak; as a result, we see the world as a constant panorama. In reality, the world we see has two holes in it, one to the right and one to the left of the center of vision.

When you look at a stone, light waves from it are changed to electro-chemical impulses by your retina, then pass on to the brain. Your brain evaluates the incoming impulses and sets up the hypothessis, "stone"; if all the information coming in supports the theory you *perceive* a stone. If, however, as you look at it, the stone becomes a bird, sprouts wings and flies, your brain is suddenly jolted into another hypothessis and has to reevaluate before it perceives properly. The brain would be much more at ease evaluating non-ambiguous information. When what seems like a stone flies, we are made uncomfortable.

If a child can look at a cow in his environment and recognize it as a cow, he perceives it. Children with reading problems have no problem in recognizing objects. This is easy to test by simply watching a child in his daily activities and listening to him. In essence, he can *read all* the physical things in his environment; he has no trouble perceiving or recognizing the actual object.

If we show him a picture of those objects he recognizes those pictures quite easily. He can, in essence, *"read" the pictures*. Pictures are not real objects, of course; they are symbols which stand for the objects, but they are closely related to the objects. The picture of a cow is easily related to a cow because the symbol, or picture, approximates what an actual cow looks like.

If a child with a reading problem easily recognizes a cow when he sees one, and he easily recognizes a picture of a cow, why then can't he recognize the written *word* "cow"? What was there about written words which made them different from the real thing or from pictures? The problem, evidently, was one of *language*.

Now I had to go back to my psychological training at the University of Pennsylvania to see if it provided a piece of the puzzle. In my studies at the Psychological Clinic, the oldest in the United States, we had studied language.

Language is a man-made *code*, composed of symbols that have no meaning in themselves. We humans have arbitrarily assigned to these symbols meanings upon which we have agreed. The word "cow" is a man-made symbol. It is in no way related to how an actual cow appears to the eye or brain. We invented or developed it as a word in the English language. It means nothing in various other languages; they have agreed on *vacca, vache, vaca, ko, kuh*—all of which mean "cow" to different groups, depending on whether their "code" is Italian, French, Spanish, Swedish, or German.

Somewhere along the line of the development of the English language the word or sound "cow" was agreed upon as the symbol to be used to represent the animal we see when we look at a cow. This agreement results in the setting up of a code of symbols to stand for things or ideas among speakers of English. To be able to use the code, one first has to memorize the meaning assigned to each symbol. If either the memory of the symbol or the memory of its assigned meaning is forgotten, the code breaks down. Thus, *storage* of both the symbol and its meaning is essential to memory.

The ability to *see* symbols is common to many levels of animal life, but *only man can store the meanings in his brain*. This ability demands a different kind of brain, and nature has handled the problem very well. The outer layer, or cortex of the human brain, is where storage takes place. Nature has split the cortex in half, down the middle from front to back, producing a right cortical hemisphere and a left cortical hemisphere. One of these hemispheres serves as the basic storage area for language information. If the hemisphere is damaged in some way, that person generally loses, to some degree, his ability to talk and read. Speech and reading are not affected if the non-language hemisphere is damaged.

Another unique phenomenon connected with this division of the human brain into language and non-language hemispheres is man's unique use of the sides of his body. Only man has developed sidedness or handedness, so that he is either right-sided or left-sided; he carries out all the skills of hand use, eye use, foot use, and ear use on the same side. If he is right-handed these functions are normally all right-sided and, if he is left-handed these functions are normally all left-sided. The splitting of the brain into a language hemisphere and non-language hemisphere serves two very important purposes. First, the information is stored efficiently and can be reacted to efficiently, since only one hemisphere deals with language. Second, having one hemisphere in control of all language and decoding functions reduces the required "wiring." The information coming in travels through superhighways right into the same area, without having to go through many tortuous side roads, which would increase both the distance and the number of avenues into the brain.

But this was very theoretical. We had no way to see it in action. Even when we looked at a live brain in the operating room it gave us no clue as to its "wiring" or its storage abilities. The only clues we got were in our before and after testing. We could see what a child could do before an operation; we knew which piece of the brain was operated on, sometimes repaired, and sometimes removed; then we could retest the child to see what effect the operation had on his ability.

We might learn more if we had a more direct way to see the brain in action. Perhaps if we had a mechanical brain, we could learn more.

These were the early days of the computer, a kind of mechanical brain. Was there some lesson to be learned from the computer's ability which might help us to better understand the human brain, since it also deals with the recognition and decoding of symbols? Like the brain, a computer is a blank at the outset. The brain needs to take things in—we call this sensory experience. The computer needs to take things in—we call this input. The computer's input consists of information, in the form of recording tapes run into the computer's nervous, or memory, system. As the tapes are played their contents are transformed into electrical energy by the computer. If this taped information were not transformed, the computer would not work. It cannot "read" or decode the information put into it unless it is in the form of electrical energy. The brain has the same problem. If there is some interference with the formation of electrical energy, then the brain cannot "read" the information going in. But, since we can easily test a child's sight, we can determine whether he is able to translate light waves into electro-chemical impulses.

The next step is the transmission of this energy. In the computer, crossed or shorted wires, inadequate connections, malfunctioning tubes or transistors can all cause a breakdown in transmitting the electrical energy. The same is true in the human brain. As each nerve pathway is used in infancy it begins to insulate itself from interference from other pathways. It becomes covered, *through use*, with a white deposit called myelin. If there is insufficient use of the pathway, it doesn't develop an adequate myelin insulation.

The third step in both the computer and the brain is *storage of information*. Decoding requires a storehouse from which information is easily retrieved. The storage areas of the computer are very precise. The same is true for the human brain. All the information needed to read or decode words is very specifically located in the brain. The more specific, the greater the ability to retrieve and to decode. Poor storage in the brain slows down the process of retrieval of information; people who suffer from this slow-down are called "deliberate" or "slow" speakers or readers. Obviously, if the incoming information is stored in an excessively disordered way, then we have a reading problem or non-reader.

Good reading, then, requires a brain (1) with the ability to change light waves into electro-chemical impulses through the visual system; (2) that has uncluttered and adequately insulated direct routes or circuits through which the electro-chemical impulses can travel efficiently; (3) with an end place where storage, retrieval, and decoding of information can take place efficiently.

We felt that perhaps some portion of reading problems in children might be reduced to one of these three categories. But, since it is a simple matter to determine whether a child can recognize objects and pictures other than words, we discarded the first and concentrated on the last two: a lack of adequate channels or circuits, and disorganized storage facilities. We were much closer to the understanding and solution of reading problems.

It was done. It had been six years since I had started with the team. Writing it was hard work because it presented a new approach to reading problems; reading problems were the result of lack of development of the nervous system, especially in the development of complete one-sidedness. The previous book relating reading to brain function was written in 1923, the year I was born, by Dr. Samuel Orton, and now I was to resurrect and add fuel to that old fire in educational circles.

I didn't care what reviewers might think of it, if it ever got published. I wondered what Glenn would think of it and, of course, if Fay decided it was not good, that was the end; and if he decided that it was good, no matter what anyone else said, it was good. Glenn was doing his afternoon stint of teaching the student nurses who now lived at the Center, learning and working with us. I waited anxiously for his break and placed the manuscript on the podium at which he was standing.

Neither of us said a word. He spent a full minute staring at the title page, "The Treatment and Prevention of Reading Problems," and then spent the remainder of the coffee break paging slowly through it.

He was misty-eyed when he looked up. I always twitted him about his Irish ancestry when he became misty-eyed, but this time I didn't. He started to talk to me but completed his statement to the student nurses, who were filing back into the room.

"This is one of the most important moments in the life of the Rehabilitation Center. Carl has finished the first book about our work. He will write many more and others will join us who will write books, so that we can move into a new era of treating all children. This is an historic moment."

I left my manuscript there and walked out. I returned to pick it up after class and Glenn asked one of the student nurses to bring in two cups of coffee, as he handed the manuscript to me.

"If we could afford it, I'd be for having scotch for a celebration, but let's celebrate anyway, with coffee," he commented.

We talked quite a while, in a glow, sitting there in the empty classroom. We were full of hope and enthusiasm. But now there were problems. Who would publish it? What would the critics say? and "My God, what will Fay say?"

We knew that it might never be published. Who had ever heard of us? It might never be reviewed; but that Fay would not react to it was impossible. We would have to wait; if he disapproved, it was a failure; if he approved, it was a success. All other reactions would be insignificant.

The next eight months went by very slowly. The book was finally accepted and now published. Fay was doing government consultation and writing; we didn't see him these days. Had he forgotten? Were we wrong in our predictions? We had been so sure that he would react—he couldn't help it.

And then it came. He said the book was good, and he obviously wrote his letter to history.

7304 Elbow Lane
Philadelphia 19, Pa.

Dr. Carl H. Delacato
Thomas Road & Northwestern Avenue
Montgomery County
Philadelphia 18, Pa.

Dear Dr. Delacato:

I have recently had time to go over your book in detail.

You have seen clearly, condensed wisely, reasoned logically, and selected from the mass of facts and data the essence that falls into sequence; your book is good.

You are to be congratulated in possessing the courage of your convictions, but more than that, admired for departing from the ancient shores of traditions; and like Columbus, anticipating and finding the lush fruits of a New World, a new way of thought and new advances in care and treatment yet to come.

I salute you as worthy of the portals of Olympus. Do not let the detracters or dissenters disturb your soul. There will forever be the *thinkers* in the high solitude of creative light, and the *stinkers* in the swarming, sweating market places of life.

You have moved from the sheltered harbor of scholastic conservatism to the open waters of the endless sea; and you still drag one anchor which must be sheathed before you unfurl the sail which will guide the way to dreamed-of shores.

Man came to speech and verbalized means of communication not by extra cortical cell layers alone (awaiting use in the more recent phylogenetic phase of developmental progress), but because of the physical contours of face, jaw, teeth, and tongue.

Which came first—the chicken or the egg? We may be sure that there *was* a *need*, and *then* a *facility!* Nature is an opportunist! Can you blame her for wanting to put "words" to "song"? (Not tonal to surds.)

Carry on; the future is what you make it—physically, mentally, and in your soul.

With warm personal regards,

(s) Temple Fay, M.D.

Chapter 5

PATTERNING THE BRAIN?

St. Martins in the Fields in Chestnut Hill is a country church. Its graceful gothic beauty is not in the least subdued by its lush surroundings of ivy and pachysandra, all kept constantly shaded by the towering maples surrounding it. Now it was subdued. Episcopalian funerals are always subdued.

It was rainy and cold on March 9, 1963. It was a Saturday and Fay was dead.

Filing into the front of the quiet church were friends of the family. I could see a few physicians sprinkled through the group —old students of Fay's. I sat in the last pew because at the back of the church were his real tribute—children of all colors, all creeds, and in all stages of rehabilitation. Some were in wheelchairs, others on crutches. Some who were learning to talk talked too loudly and disturbed the hushed church. They all moved around a bit too much.

Their very ability to move around and their new disturbing voices were a tribute to Fay—who helped give them these abilities. The children wriggled in their wheel chairs, some tried to make the sign of the cross, others looked around through vacant eyes. They were quiet only when the hymns were sung. They liked the music.

I didn't listen to the eulogy. I had my own. Fay had made many contributions to medicine, such as fluid control to help brain-injured patients improve more rapidly, carbon dioxide therapy to help the brain receive more nourishment, and human refrigeration which was to make possible great future advances in surgery. But his greatest contribution was his view of the human brain. He was not only a brilliant neurosurgeon, he understood the brain. His evolutionary theory of brain development and his theory of treatment were criticized by many. One well known, but completely naive, critic had stated, "I'd like to see one of his patients try to creep down Fifth Avenue." Fay never showed disappointment; he was always kind to these critics, never giving up hope that he would eventually convince them.

In the pew across from me a hyperactive, brain-injured little boy, one of our patients who couldn't walk or talk, slid down off his mother's lap and crept on the church floor toward me. As he crept closer he noticed who I was and smiled up at me broadly, from his hands and knees. I tried to smile back but the only thing I could do was cry, not because I was sad but because the world had been so unfair to a great genius. If that kid could creep in a church, maybe some day he would *walk* down Fifth Avenue.

Now we were completely alone. No longer did we have Fay as our mentor, teacher, or even conscience. Bob, Glenn, and I talked very little about Fay's death.

Increasing numbers of patients and students arrived at the Center. Meetings of the Board of Directors were constantly taken up by discussion of the problems of patients waiting for admission. Finally, one board member suggested that "since children seem so important to you and since children have more years before them, perhaps you should no longer treat adults." Our lives were changing rapidly. Children began coming to us from many parts of the country.

We were now so busy that I had to face a new decision, to leave Chestnut Hill Academy. There was no question about my decision, for I had not even thought about that headmastership in a plush, private school for a long time; all I had thought about since 1952 was the possibility of finding a real solution to reading problems.

A large foundation grant made available to us the building next door, now doubling our campus to fourteen acres with two mansions. We added buildings as they were needed and as they could be afforded. The staff was now composed of fifty hard-working and bright young people.

With children our only patients, we even changed our name. We weren't really rehabilitating them, because they had never been habilitated. We needed a name which would indicate that we were working to help each of them to use as much of the brain as possible. We finally decided on the name, "The Institutes for the Achievement of Human Potential." We called it Institutes because now there were several divisions, including departments of Research and Clinical Investigation.

Now we spent all our time with children. We studied a number of normal babies to see if we could trace the development of handedness and of language hemispheres. We saw immediately that infants under the age of one have no handedness, they are quite ambidextrous, and they have little, if any, speech. We could only conclude that we are not born with a definite handedness; it develops. As it develops with age and experience, does it, in turn, develop the brain? Was it possible that we had looked at the brain in reverse? We had assumed that functions and performance were the *result* of brain development. Was it possible that brain development was the *result* of functions and performance? For instance, we had assumed that a healthy brain made it possible to walk, but could it be that the process of going through the stages toward walking is what created the complete and intact brain? If it were possible that the brain was the *result* of body use instead of the *cause*, then we had opened a whole new field, in which we had five avenues into the brain and five possible ways of changing it: seeing, hearing, feeling through touching, tasting, and smelling. We now began to experiment with these channels in an effort to see if we could possibly change the brain. Our most exciting experiment was with movement.

Fay had taught us his evolutionary theory. He used the development of man to build his theory. Fay saw the stages man's brain went through (fish, amphibian, reptile, to mammal) as the guide posts to development. We were more interested in the development of a single human being from birth on. Did he also go through stages of development?

Most of the severely brain-injured children who came to us could not walk; in fact, if placed on the floor on their stomachs most of them could not move. It would be hopeless to try to teach a child to walk if he could not move his body from one spot to another, when placed on the floor. A baby, at birth, can move its arms and legs but can't move from one place to another, and it is also impossible to teach a newborn baby to walk. We wondered why other animals walked immediately or shortly after birth. Why did humans need a year before they walked?

The only answer seemed to be that they needed to go through stages to *prepare* them to walk. We began to study the development of movement in normal newborn babies and we found that they first start moving from place to place on their stomachs, using wriggling trunkal movements. Next they begin to crawl using one side of the body at a time to push the body along while the tummy remains in contact with the floor. They then get up on their hands and knees and creep, using two sides of the body. Only after this do they begin to stand. We found even walking went through stages, beginning with holding on to furniture, then becoming a poorly balanced and somewhat dangerous activity in which the arms are used as balance poles and finally developing into normal walking.

What would happen if we combined our new knowledge with Fay's idea of patterning? He had never been able to use patterning as a long-term, intensive treatment. If we patterned a child who couldn't crawl through the crawling motions each day for months, perhaps his brain would learn how it feels to crawl. If he could learn how it *feels* to crawl, this learning would have to go through existing but unused channels of the brain, or it even might create new channels. If the children did learn how it *feels* to crawl, this learning had to be *stored* some place in the brain.

We selected a few such severely brain-injured children and moved their limbs through the crawling motions. This required three adults, one holding the head and one on each side moving the arms and legs in the crawling motion, a process Fay had called "patterning." The hope was that we were impressing on the brain the pattern of the movements required for crawling, and that the brain might respond by *learning* how it felt to crawl.

The next hope was that a brain which knew how it felt to crawl would then choose to *command* these crawling motions to be done and the child would crawl by himself. Patterning involved untold hours of hard physical labor all of which, we had to admit, seemed aimed at a very illusive goal.

When the first brain-injured child we had patterned for months began to crawl around spontaneously when placed on the floor and left to his own devices, we were overjoyed! As time went by, a number of other brain-injured children began to crawl after varying periods of crawling stimulation.

Next, we devised patterns for creeping (which takes place on hands and knees) and the same thing happened. After enough pouring in of the creeping pattern some brain-injured children began to creep when placed on the floor. We seemed to be successfully forcing new channels into the brain, or setting up new information storage areas. Perhaps the brain could be changed more than we had dreamed, if we worked hard enough.

Now was the time for a more critical test of our theory. It had long been known that through lack of use various parts of the body and nervous system fail to develop. As early as 1896 experiments were conducted showing that if at birth one eye of a rat is sewn closed, the other, unclosed and seeing eye develops an insulating myelin sheath on the optic nerve much more rapidly than the non-seeing eye. Use and stimulation resulted in changes of the nervous system.

Some severely brain-injured children arrived at the Institutes blind. Examination of their eyes indicated that their eyes were much like those of infants, and often we could not find in the eyes themselves any specific reason for the blindness. Since the eyes appeared unused but relatively normal, we conjectured that perhaps these brain-injured children could not see because they had inadequate channels into the brain for seeing; in effect, perhaps these brain-injured children could not see because they had never *learned* to see. The brain injury might have changed the brain enough so that the injured brain needed, but failed to get, an *extra* amount of activity to create the proper neural channels for seeing. Could we put into this hurt brain a pattern for seeing which might develop or make usable channels in the brain? Would giving the child a more complete visual stimulation result in his learning to see?

We exposed these blind brain-injured children to light in a sequence, starting with white light flooding the room for five seconds, alternating with five seconds of darkness. We next placed various brightly colored lights about the walls of the room to which we attached various loud sounds. Whenever a light went on its loud sound accompanied it. We were not surprised that some children never learned to follow the lights and sounds, but we were delighted with those who first learned to follow the light-sound combination, and then a few followed the lights alone! The children who could follow the lights without the sound had learned to see! They had developed brain channels that now enabled them to see various colored lights. We continued to change the stimulus as we treated them, and many continued to develop better vision. A few of this original group of blind children went on to visual reading and school!

Glenn and I wrote to Veras, who had returned to Brazil, about our findings. He wrote back in English that he was thrilled. No longer was he an eye-surgeon; he had formed an

Institute modeled on ours. It was delightful to have an ex-eye-surgeon congratulate us on our experiments in vision.

We missed Veras; his son had done better than we had hoped. He could use his arms; his legs were still quite weak, but he was now in college taking pre-med.

Bob and I had been envious a few months earlier as we put Glenn on the plane to Rio to officiate at the opening of Veras's new Institute. Glenn's reports of the new Institute and the wonderful Brazilians were intriguing. Veras insisted that Bob and I had to come. He sent me a personal message: "I am glad that Carl is finally learning something about vision and perception."

Veras was one of the earliest student protestors and, irritatingly, one of the best.

Our experiments had now convinced us that we could influence the development of the brain by stimulating it. We soon learned that if we stimulated feeling, sight, and sound at the same time the whole process was speeded. This was the last piece of evidence we needed to set up our theory of reading.

We had learned that reading was the result of an eye-brain relationship and that the brain was the most important element in the process. We knew that if the brain was changed (either surgically or by accident), reading changed. We had also learned that if the use of some parts of the body were changed, reading changed. We had theorized, and proved to our satisfaction, that deliberately changing the use of some parts of the body could affect the brain. Everyone accepts the fact that greater use of other parts of the body, such as muscles, develops bigger and stronger muscles. Consider, for instance, the weight lifter. Why shouldn't it, therefore, be true that the *brain also develops through use!*

Changing theory into practice is difficult. Happily, we had a bright and eager staff. They helped to create practical applications of our theories. People came to learn from many parts of the world. They began to call our treatment the Doman-Delacato treatment. This was meant as a high compliment, but it was also the beginning of making us more controversial than we had ever dreamed possible. Their attaching our names to these ideas must have given the opposition a fright, because clouds of suspicion began to form among our peers, who were also our competition.

We had more to learn. Since the brain is so rapidly and constantly developing and changing in a growing child, it is difficult to see or understand what *pattern* this development follows. This is not as true with severely brain-injured children, for the injury slows the brain's normally rapid development. If it is severe enough, it stops development. A good deal can be learned about the normal patterns by watching the development of brain-injured children, since it generally follows, in slow motion, the same over-all plan as normal development.

After studying hundreds of these slow-motion developers, we were able finally to gain new insights and, as we worked, a pattern began to appear; we were learning in fascinating detail how the human nervous system develops.

We learned that the human nervous system develops through use, and that the opportunity for use provided to children is therefore directly related to this development. The brain actually grows through use. One way to measure this growth and development is to study the myelinization, which is the formation of the white sheath covering the nerve fibers. Many such studies had already been carried out on animals.

Klosovskii in Russia, for instance, studied cats from the same litter. He allowed one-half of the litter a normal life and placed the other half of the litter on a small rotating device at twenty-four to thirty-six hours of age. They were just rocked back and forth for a number of hours per day. The theory was that, if the use of the brain develops myelinization, this rocking activity would increase the myelinization in the balance centers of the brain. After ten to nineteen days Klosovskii found that the cats which had been rocked had up to thirty-five percent more myelinization in the balance centers of the brain than did their non-rocking brothers and sisters.*

At the University of California, in Berkeley, a group of scientists headed by Krech studied the plasticity and growth of the brain. They have found that when mice are stimulated through the senses their brains grow larger and weigh more than those of their litter mates who have not been so stimulated. They found that when vision is stimulated, there is a great increase in the size and weight of the visual areas of the brains, compared to the non-stimulated group. The same thing happened in experiments on rats. Given an environment which contains more stimulation, the rats developed a greater weight and thickness of brain tissue and an increase in the brain's chemical activities.

We next reduced the patterns of development which we now finally understood to what we considered the six most basic areas. Three of these areas are *reception*, or intake: *seeing*, culminating in reading; *hearing*, culminating in understanding spoken language; and *feeling*, with the skin and muscles, culminating in recognition of objects by feeling them. (We did not include taste and smell because they didn't appear to be basic to the problems of the children whom we were seeing.) Three others are *output*: *moving*, culminating in walking; *production* of sound, culminating in talking; and *hand use*, culminating in writing. We found that most of the development of the human nervous system is accomplished through these six channels—three in and three out, each one reenforcing the others.

We found that the three "in" channels—feeling, hearing, and seeing—each develops in its own sequence and that each one was important to brain development. We also found that the "out" channels of mobility, speech, and hand use, depended upon the "in" channels. We found that these six channels continued to develop through infancy and childhood, and that a lack of opportunity for development of *any one* of these channels had

* For an excellent description of this and many other similar studies see *The Development of the Brain and Its Disturbance by Harmful Factors* by B. N. Klosovskii, Macmillan, 1963.

an effect upon the development of the others. Each of the six channels goes through its own developmental stages, depending upon the age of the child and his experience, and each stage is important to the final product. We found the old saying, that you have to creep before you can walk, is good sense. Each of these areas goes through a developmental sequence, and if one stage of the sequence is neglected, the whole channel is affected. Gesell, the pioneer in the field of development, had been over this path before us, but we were looking through new eyes and we discovered new and exciting information about human development; we had found a pattern.

The child with the reading problem must, we concluded, have a brain that is different in some way from that of the normal reader. If we could find the differences in brain development between the two, we would have finally located the real cause of the reading problem, and if we could change that brain's development we could solve the reading problem. We finally knew what to look for.

We surrounded ourselves with hundreds of children of all ages with reading problems and looked for a whole new world of things which they might have in common. We looked for signs of *brain dysfunction* or a *lack of brain development*. We found that the things they had in common were:

1. They seemed to lack coordination. We watched them walk and run, and they lacked grace. We watched their creeping and crawling to see if just walking and running were poorly developed. We found that they were equally poor in creeping and crawling.

2. They had great difficulty in deciding to be right- or left-handed, as do many five- and six-year-olds. Many of them still had difficulty in deciding which hand to use, even though well beyond age six. This also carried over into foot use and eye use. If asked to kick a ball, they would run up to it and then often hesitate because they

could not decide which foot to use. When asked to aim a rifle, they would, many times, aim it right-handed and then twist their necks around so that they awkwardly sighted with the left eye. Given a telescope to look through, they tended to look through it with the opposite eye from the writing hand.

3. About twenty percent of them wrote or threw a ball with their left hands. This was almost three times as many left-handers as we find among good readers and in the normal population.

4. They seemed to love music and to derive more pleasure from listening to music than did their brothers and sisters.

5. Their handwriting had no consistency of slant. When we looked at a page of their handwriting, the vertical lines of the letters, such as "h,j,p,t,l," made all kinds of different angles.

6. Even though most had normal eyes when tested, they all seemed to have some difficulty seeing efficiently. As a result, almost all of them held their heads much too close to the book when attempting to read, many practically touching their noses to the paper when writing.

7. A large number of them tended to read or write backwards: "was" for "saw" or "42" for "24," in the second and third grades. Many first graders do this but it disappears with normal readers. It did not disappear in the reading problems. This is probably why, historically, children who had trouble learning to read were called backward.

8. Most were poor spellers. Some could learn a list of spelling words as homework and pass a test the next day. Two days later they acted as though they had never seen the words before.

9. Many seemed to do better in arithmetic than in reading, and they all did better in discussion than in writing.

10. Every one of them had much better language comprehension through their ears than through their eyes.

We next tested two hundred normal readers and found that they *did not* have these problems. We had finally isolated the factors which poor readers had in common. They related to the development of the nervous system.

We had to learn a great deal more about the development of the human nervous system. We knew that we had just begun to scratch the surface, that there was so much more to be learned. But it was a true beginning.

We had just taken off from Belem, on the equator, for the final leg of our journey to Rio. Glenn sat on the window side of the plane looking out over the muddy Amazon and the impenetrable blue-green jungle surrounding it. He stared for a long time. He didn't look at me but seemed to talk to the window. "Carl, how strongly do you believe that kids are harmed if they skip a stage of development?"

"Very," I answered.

Still looking out the window at the jungle, he asked, "Carl, how strongly do you believe that many of the reading problems you see are caused by missing the creeping stage?"

I shouldn't have answered because it sounded like a trap, but I did anyway, "Very."

It was a trap. "We can prove or disprove our theory down there. No parent would put a child on the ground in that jungle, what with poisonous insects and snakes, poisonous plants, and wild animals. I suspect that no child ever crawls or creeps down there. Everybody down there should have a reading problem if our theory is right. We must see."

Glenn slept as we flew over the remaining thousand miles of jungle. I hoped he was dreaming about comfortable Chestnut Hill, or delightful Rio, and not about whether kids crawl or creep in the jungle. He wasn't, for in the very near future we were to fight through those jungles below us, many times.

Chapter 6

TALKING, WRITING, READING

We saw thousands of children.

The puzzle of how a child develops was becoming clearer. The difficulty was in finding which of the developmental stages were important stages and which were not. We were beginning to learn more about how children's nervous systems matured and what was required for total development.

As a newborn begins the dramatic process of learning how to use his nervous system, thereby developing it, he goes through four basic stages. Each of the stages is necessary to total development. If one stage is short-changed by lack of opportunity, the end result will be affected and the brain development will be incomplete; it will have areas which are not properly developed. The result will be a somewhat "unfinished" human being, which is another way of describing a reading problem.

The first stage of brain development takes place between birth and six months of age. Spencer wrote that the newborn is a "white paper" upon which experience makes its mark. This could aptly describe the newborn's nervous system. He does not see; he must *learn* to see. We must all recover from infant blindness. At birth the baby's eyes are bluish gray and almost mature in size. They can barely make out light and dark and their motions are quite uncontrolled. The eyes tend to roll around in a meaningless fashion in relation to one another. After ten days of looking, he learns to pick out objects in space with at least one eye at a time. This important object in space is usually mother. If he has no contrasting light and dark, he does not learn to see.

He has to learn to hear. The sound of his mother talking to him, even though he obviously doesn't understand her words, is teaching his brain to hear. The voices of the other members of the family, the radio and television, traffic, and so on, are all necessary if he is to develop the brain channels for hearing which will later enable him to hear and understand speech.

He has to learn to feel, just as did the animals in the experiments of Klosovskii and Krech, in order to develop the brain channels which will later be required for moving his body efficiently. The feel of his bath, his mother's arms, his blanket, a towel—all contribute to the development of his nervous system at this stage. Anything which limits sensory opportunity at this time is limiting the development of required brain channels. It could be the beginning of the creation of an incompletely developed nervous system.

At this time the visual apparatus is ready to go into action; that is, it is ready for the child to learn. During the first three months of life, the most basic approach to reading begins. The child, at this stage, needs a great deal of visual stimulation. Learning to see is closely associated with movement, head position, and the use of all the other senses.

Some interesting experiments have been carried out to study these relationships. One of the most ingenious studies was conducted by Held, who brought up kittens in darkness from birth allowing them to see only during the experiments. One kitten was placed in a basket with his head uncovered and his legs sticking out and touching the floor so that he could turn the basket around by using his legs. The other kitten was placed in a basket with only his head uncovered so that he could see, but he couldn't move his legs. His basket was connected to the first by a pulley, so that, when the first kitten moved, the second moved in the same direction and traveled the same distance. The only difference was that one kitten's legs were touching the floor and turning the basket and the other kitten's legs were not being used at all. Held found that the kitten which was allowed to use his legs to create movement learned to see and to perceive. The other kitten, who had the identical visual experience but who did not use his legs, remained unable to see effectively. This was a dramatic demonstration of the fact that learning to see required movement of body.

We became convinced that a baby should be given every opportunity for movement at this stage, not only for movement's sake, but also to help vision develop more completely. Restrictive clothes or restrictive chairs, cribs, and playpens do not help to encourage movement. It is interesting that mothers seem always to have sensed this need for movement, a fact evident in the habit of most mothers, while playing with infants, of "exercising" them gently.

In order to stimulate his visual development at this stage the baby should not be left alone for long periods of time while awake. Parents have, in the past, been prone to be overly quiet and quite inactive with new babies, but keeping baby in an unstimulating, serene environment is not helpful to his development. He should be put in a position where he can actively survey his environment, and to some extent become involved in it.

We can't wait until six years of age to teach a child to perceive. The process of learning to see, which precedes learning to perceive and is followed by learning to read, must begin at birth. The child who cannot read has not developed his perceptual skills to the degree that he can differentiate between small visual symbols, which we call written words. He has not used and, therefore, has not developed the eye, the optic nerves, and the brain to the point where he can deal efficiently with the visual world around him. He must also be exposed to likenesses and differences in all kinds of sounds so that he can learn to discriminate among them. Only then can he begin to comprehend music or sound, or, indeed, speech. If the child is unable to hear correctly from early infancy he will have difficulty learning to talk. If he is not exposed to enough or varied enough sounds to hear, he will also have difficulty in learning to talk well, simply because his hearing apparatus is not sophisticated enough for him to deal with what is going into his brain. Hearing activities begin their development at a very low level of the brain, the foundation upon which subsequent brain levels develop.

We learned that the three "in" and the three "out" channels cannot develop in isolation. They *must* be used together. The "out" channels help to reenforce the "in" channels and they must coordinate if they are to develop the brain to its fullest potential. Vision without hearing and mobility is incomplete; mobility without vision and hearing is incomplete; hearing without mobility and vision is incomplete. The brain needs to have them used simultaneously, just as they will be later in life, in order to profit fully from their use.

Opportunity is the keynote at this stage of development. Opportunities to see, hear, feel, move, use hands and arms, and vocalize, all make a contribution to the development of the nervous system. The opportunity to do all of them simultaneously is the first goal of this stage, which in turn sets up differentiation of function, and it also sets the stage for an increasingly complex relationship among these six activities.

As soon as the baby's brain is able to deal with these channels simultaneously he begins automatically and, in part reflexly, to experiment with specialization of various brain sections. Luria, in Russia, describes this as the organization of functional systems. Even though this takes place at a low level, it is the real beginning of specialized patterns of brain functions, and the process makes itself visible in his use of one side of the body at a time.

The one-sided pattern is generally first seen in movement. The earliest crawling movements are one-sided; that is, as the baby tries to crawl on his stomach, he pulls up his right arm and right leg and uses them to move his body forward; on the next try, he pulls up his left arm and left leg and uses them to move forward. He is learning to use one side of his body at a time, alternating the side so that when one side is active the other side is at rest. This is also true for the brain; as one side is active, the other side is relatively inactive. With each move the infant also turns his head toward the forward or active hand. Alternate turning of the head forces the eyes and ears of the child into new patterns of perception since they are also alternated with each move.

If you watch an infant crawl, you will note that he has no choice about this because one eye is against the crawling surface and is blocked from use by that surface. As the next push takes place, the head turns, freeing the blocked eye for sight. With this alternation of head position the baby is, in essence, setting up very crude pathways to his brain. It is the very simple beginning of proper visual stimulation through the correct channels into the proper portion of the brain.

The same is true for the ears. As the infant turns his head to face the alternate left and right hands—and the eye is closed by the contact with the mattress—the ear on that side is also blocked by its contact with the mattress. As he looks at his left hand, before he pushes with it, his right eye is against the mattress and is not used and his right ear is also blocked by the mattress. When he turns his head on the next push and looks at his right hand, then his left eye and ear become blocked by the mattress. Movement, hand and leg use, hearing, and vision are all combined in this alternating pattern as the baby crawls. As a result, the brain is being developed to take in all these activities simultaneously and it also is learning to do so one side at a time.

The brain goes through two very basic developments at this stage. First is the ability to change the stimulation which comes to it in the form of light waves, sound waves, and touch into electro-chemical energy with which the brain can deal both *individually* and *simultaneously*. Without this basic ability further development of the nervous system would be most difficult.

The second development which emerges at this stage is the earliest form of brain specialization, the pattern of *alternate* operation of each side of the brain, for the activities of moving, hearing, seeing, and feeling. This separation of the functions of both sides of the body prepares the brain to move on to the next stage.

Generally, the second stage of brain development takes place between six months and one year of age. It is characterized by a very different pattern. Instead of using brain and body in alternate one-sidedness, the baby now learns to use parts of both sides of his body *together* in a predetermined way, which we have called a *cross pattern*. He no longer crawls on his stomach, using only one side of his body at a time but, using alternate sides of his body for propulsion, he now *creeps* on his hands and knees. As he creeps, the *opposite* hand and knee are used simultaneously, the right knee and left hand, then the left knee and right hand. His eyes and ears are now used very differently because the head is no longer in contact with the surface on which he is moving, his trunk is now up in the air, resting or moving, on the alternate hand and knee in a *cross pattern*. See Photos 3, 4, and 5.

At this stage the infant learns to use both eyes together. He no longer takes in the world one eye at a time. His brain now begins to develop the ability to take in two separate visual sensations at one time and to convert them into a single perception. This requires a more complex brain circuitry and is the basis of depth perception.

The same is true for hearing. The infant begins to use his two ears together and his brain begins to put together the sensations coming to it from each ear and to deal with them simultaneously. As a result of his new brain channels and of his new two-sided brain activity, he now begins to locate sounds in space. Mother's voice, or other interesting sounds coming from various directions, help him to develop these abilities at this stage.

During this stage a great deal of movement and much creeping about is necessary if the brain channels are to be completely developed. As shown with Held's and Klosovskii's experiments, using the body for mobility helps to reenforce the development of the visual portions of the brain, and to strengthen the use of two eyes and two ears.

At this time not only do the eyes begin to work together, but the hands and eyes begin to operate in unison. The baby needs to do much exploring; visual activity accompanied by sound and touch should be encouraged. His crib should actually be moved about once each week; the headboard should be against the wall, with both sides free, so that he can enjoy as much seeing as possible. Anyone entering the room should talk so that the infant will look in his direction. Mother should talk whenever moving about the room to help the infant to discover the third dimension of both sound and sight. Here again, opportunity for seeing and hearing is the keynote to development.

Without adequate opportunity to creep about, and without adequate stimulation to the ears and eyes the necessary brain development remains incomplete. As the brain experiences these activities, it develops efficient channels which prepare it for the next stage of development.

Children generally enter the third stage of development between one year and eighteen months of age. At this time they begin to make use of the outer surface of the brain, the *cortex,* more exclusively. This surface is the "gray matter"; it has many creases and fissures which provide it with an extremely large surface. The stage is characterized by the beginning of uniquely human activities of walking and talking.

The child makes his first attempts to become upright during this stage. He begins by pulling himself up onto his feet while holding on to furniture. This new upright position gives him a whole new world in which the balance requirements are quite different; his hand use is different, and even the world he hears becomes different. As he adjusts to these differences and gains courage, he begins to imitate those around him and walks. His first steps are unsafe, but very exciting. He uses his arms as balance poles. As he improves, he begins to walk in a more stable and graceful pattern. (Graceful walking is the result of graceful creeping; both consist of the same basic cross-pattern motions.) In graceful human walking, as the right foot moves forward the left arm moves forward serving as a counterbalance, and on the next step as the left foot moves forward the right arm moves forward, also as a counterbalance. This is easy to see if you stand on a street corner and watch people walking by. Notice the rhythm of arm and leg swing as they walk by. The movements are the same as those of cross-pattern creeping, except that creeping is on the hands and knees and walking is upright.

The child at this stage continues to use both sides of his brain; the real difference from the previous stage is that, for the first time in his development, he is in a human upright position. The upright position places new demands on his developing brain. Balance becomes much more important, and it is intertwined with the seeing and hearing channels of the brain. Without seeing and hearing perfect balance is impossible, and without balance perfect seeing and hearing are impossible. As balance improves the development of the eye-brain and ear-brain channels changes. Being in an upright position allows the child to see a world at greater distance, and depth becomes more important in vision. To see in depth the child's brain must fuse the two pictures, coming from the two eyes, into one image and must make sense out of it. Since he is now walking and moving from side to side his brain must begin to fuse the pictures coming from each eye at a *very rapid rate*. At this stage the child is exposed to many new visual experiences and with each his brain develops.

If we examine the visual experiences we give to children at this age we find that we allow them to look at all sorts of objects and pictures, but we normally do not expose them to written words until the age of six. As a result, the visual channels are developed during this stage to deal with all sorts of visual activities except words.

The child begins to take in sounds from both ears and learns to put them together. In essence, he learns to hear stereophonically. If we examine what sounds we expose him to during this stage we find that, while he is exposed to all sorts of sounds, the most consistent are spoken words or human speech. The child's world is surrounded by the spoken word, but as a rule he is not exposed to the written word until much later in his development.

We begin to see that the opportunity for the development of ear-brain relationships is quite different from the opportunity for eye-brain relationships. The child is learning to decode verbal abstractions through his ears but *not* through his eyes. For many children this difference tends to slow the development of the visual area. The visual area needs a great amount of stimulation at this time both in handling abstractions beyond pictures, and exposure to written words in large form, which will make it possible for him to become familiar with written words. Television commercials have given children an excellent opportunity to see written words in large form at an early age, and happily there are fewer children each year who are suffering from this lack of experience.

By the end of the third stage the baby is walking upright, understanding some words, saying a word or two, and has mastered both the specialized and simultaneous use of the two sides of his brain and body. He has also progressed from using very low brain levels up to and including the human or outer portion of the brain.

He is now ready to move on to the final and uniquely human stage of brain development which begins between eighteen months and two years of age. This final stage is usually completed by six or seven years of age, and results in complete one-sidedness—that is, one of the two halves of the brain becomes dominant and takes over as the language hemisphere.

Complete "sidedness" (habitual use of foot, hand, and eye on the same side of the body) occurs only in human beings, who are the only creatures who can read, write, and talk. Lower forms of animals, such as primates, develop up to this stage, but stop short here. They never develop this uniquely human characteristic of sidedness, with one-half of the cortex becoming the dominant, language-controlling hemisphere, and the other becoming sub-dominant.

As a result of having sidedness, man has a spoken and written language. Many scientists have wondered why man alone has developed sidedness, how and when he first acquired it, and there have been a number of fascinating attempts to explain it. Some anthropologists feel that man first developed sidedness when he began to make and use tools. Others are of the opinion that the use by early man of weapons and shields for protection in battle was the significant factor. Still others feel that his upright posture allowed him to free his hands and to use one side exclusively as a matter of efficiency, or that ancient tribal or religious rites have influenced the establishment of sidedness in man, or that dominance of one hemisphere of the brain over another simply was an inevitable outcome of biological evolution.

Although the reason for the origin of sidedness in man is not certain, there is general agreement that it exists in man alone, and there is some agreement that language and sidedness appeared on the evolutionary scene at about the same time. It is known that there is a cross-over in the brain which results in the left half controlling the right side of the body and the right half controlling the left side of the body. In humans who learn to read and write, one of these halves must become dominant, that is, become the hemisphere that controls skills. If the left half of the brain becomes dominant, the child becomes right-handed; he should also become right-footed, right-eared, and right-eyed. If the right half of the brain becomes dominant, the child should become left-handed, left-footed, left-eared, and left-eyed. The dominant half of the brain becomes the language center. Here is where reading, writing, talking, and the learning of language are controlled. Here is where reading and the decoding of speech take place, as well as the storage of language. *If one of the halves does not become dominant, then the brain is not completely developed and a problem with reading usually results.*

Ambidexterity, generally, is a warning sign of future difficulty with reading. Mixed-sidedness also signals trouble; this means that all of the impulses are not going to a single dominant hemisphere and the ability to decode, or read, will be affected. Children at this stage, however, must not be forced toward one side or another. When they have made their own natural choice of sidedness, they must be helped to become completely one-sided—right or left—whichever it is. If a child is ambidextrous at this stage, he will probably not develop a skilled dominant eye. As the small visual symbols, which we call words, go into his brain through the eye they are controlled as perceptions in only one hemisphere of the brain. But if, because of his lack of a dominant eye, they register on both hemispheres, the child will tend to read backwards, to "mirror" his writing. The effort here must be to make one eye dominant, then the reversals in reading tend to disappear.

Children should be helped to be one-sided in terms of handedness. As their handedness becomes more established, their eyedness usually follows and they then are able to deal with smaller perceptions and more sophisticated differentiations because, as the perception goes into the dominant eye, it is controlled in the dominant cortical hemisphere.

Since the great majority of humans are right-sided (estimates vary between 80 percent to 95 percent being right-handed), the emphasis has been to encourage right-handedness and to discourage left-handedness. This is reflected in many languages where the word for right shows preference or means *correct*, as it does in English, and the word for left is much more negative. Happily, however, this attitude toward left-handers is changing and we are no longer forcing handedness on children, as we did in the past. Studies show that ten to fifteen percent of our general population is genetically biased toward, or ordained to be, left-handed. Such children should be allowed to be left-handed; the others should be allowed to be right-handed. There should be no forcing of choice. When the child has indicated a strong preference, every encouragement should be given to him to operate completely with that side as the skilled or dominant side.

There have been numerous cases of children whose handedness was changed by parents and, as a result, these children became severe reading problems. There are also numerous instances where a change in handedness has caused stuttering. What happens is that the two halves of the brain become so finely balanced that both sides attempt to become language hemispheres. In the resulting conflict over storage and retrieval of the coded information, the child begins to stutter or to reverse in his reading.

Another interesting change occurs as children begin to develop a dominant hemisphere. All of the language skills go into the language hemisphere, but, conversely, the musical skills in the form of listening to it, as well as singing, begin to move into the other, or sub-dominant hemisphere.* We feel that a child should have an abundance of music until the age of five. At this time a gradual decrease of the amount of music in the environment should take place, to allow the language hemisphere to become dominant.

By now, we had learned that in order to become a normal reading, writing, and talking human being each child had to start at birth with a reasonably intact nervous system. From birth on, as we have seen, the nervous system and brain develop through four basic stages. The first is the stage of crawling and the use of opposite sides of the body alternately; it is a very low and simple brain stage. Creeping on hands and knees and the

---

* Research has been carried out at the Montreal Neurological Institute indicating that the sub-dominant hemisphere is usually the seat of tonal activity. For an excellent review of this and other research on brain function, see *Cognitive Processes and the Brain* by Milner and Glickman, Van Nostrand, 1965.

use of the two sides of the body simultaneously are learned during the second stage. Here the brain learns to govern arms, legs, eyes, ears, and hands at the same time. During the third stage, the outer layer of the brain comes into greater use. It is the beginning of the stage. Now, walking and talking appear. The brain develops and early human behavior results. During the fourth and final stage one-half of this outer layer of brain becomes dominant and the child develops complete one-sidedness.

We had come a long way in our studies and we knew our conclusions were valid. Fortunately, at the same time other researchers were also concerned with the development of the nervous system.

Hebb, in Canada, had postulated a theoretical model of brain development. Ashby, of England, had clearly defined his design for a brain. Other scientists, such as Krech, at the University of California, studied the effects of enriched and deprived environments on the growth of the brain. Dart, from South Africa, was adding new insights through his great knowledge of comparative anatomy, and Held, at M.I.T., had demonstrated new relationships of movement to nervous system development.

The Russians, whose scientists have long been interested in the development of the brain, were led by Luria, who worked on the restoration of function after brain injury, and Klosovskii, with his monumental experiments on the brain development of cats.

Most of the research which went on was concentrated on animals, but each new finding helped us at the Institutes to see a bit more clearly the pattern of development of the human nervous system.

The brain was no longer held captive in a prison of bone.

Chapter 7

PRIMITIVE MAN

AUGUST, 1966 was clear and cool in the Kalahari Desert of what was then Bechuanaland, and is now Botswana. After two weeks of living with the very primitive and nomadic Bushmen, it would be pleasant to return to Johannesburg. Sleeping under the stars on the desert floor, eating small game, living with the beguiling Bushmen children, was exciting and fun; but after two weeks, one misses a bath and enough water to brush one's teeth. These luxuries were awaiting us in Johannesburg.

I'd never felt cleaner than I did as Glenn and I walked into the University of Witwattersrand. We were to see once again the Dean Emeritus of the Medical School, famed Raymond A. Dart, before commencing our four thousand mile trek north to Nairobi.

Professor Dart greeted us warmly, as he met us in a hall under a sign which read, "the Dart Memorial Museum." As he led us down the hall he put an arm around each of us and said in his crisp accent, "Glenn and Carl, you don't look any worse for wear. How were the Bush babies?"

We reported briefly on our trip to the Kalahari. Bushmen children were never allowed on the ground, they tested like our reading problems, and they have no written language.

At the end of the corridor we turned left into a small office which contained a large safe. Today we would see it! The skull and petrified brain which Professor Dart had found in 1923, the year I was born, and with which he started the uproar that made him the man to whom science would be apologizing for the next century. When Dart proposed in 1925 that this was a human skull and that man was not a mere 100,000 years old born in Asia, but was, instead, over a million years old and born in Africa, the scientific world was astounded. In fact, for thirty years the scientific world rejected completely Dart's early man, whom he had named Australopithecus. Later finds and carbondating techniques proved Dart to have been correct. Recently Dart's book, *Adventures with the Missing Link,* and Robert Ardrey's popular *African Genesis* had made Dart not only the world's most renowned anthropological discoverer, but also a symbol to all men of science who differed with the establishment. He had persevered and he had won.

It was thrilling to hold the skull and petrified brain in my hands, to see how Dart had chipped away the limestone with his wife's knitting needles. I passed it along to Glenn very carefully. I thought back to 1952, when Glenn had handed me the first brain I had ever seen in a jar.

"It's a great thrill, sir. I'm sure that all those years of rejection were made easier by having this brain to look at," I said to Dart. He smiled, "It was by no means always easy, Carl."

Although seventy-three, Dart was full of energy and activity, almost hyperactivity. He in South Africa and Fay in Philadelphia had many of the same ideas about the evolving human brain. Sadly, they had never met. Dart's great knowledge of the human brain was the only reason he could make his now famed deductions about the emergence of man from looking at a skull and a petrified brain.

Dart's unique knowledge of the brain was what had brought us to see him originally. We had some continuing failures with certain kinds of children. We needed more knowledge of the development of man's brain. Dart was a leading authority on comparative anatomy and he had spent thirty years fighting his critics by learning more and more about how the human brain evolved. We needed his knowledge. The United Steelworkers of America had agreed to pay Dart's salary at the Institutes if we could entice him away from Africa.

Dinner with Dart and his effervescent, charming wife, Marjorie, was a delight. Dart's tales of inacceptance of his ideas, told in his unique turn of phrase, coupled with his native Australian accent, sounded like yarns from a story book. I kept wondering about this man all through dinner. How could he have lived with so much rejection and ridicule? How could he have worked for thirty years in the face of such overwhelming odds? How could he fight the gray beards of England and the United States for so long and still be able to tell charming stories about the very people who rejected and ridiculed?

I would wait for the bitterness to show, if not in him, perhaps in Marjorie. In all the years I was to know this blue-eyed couple with their distinctive accents, never once was I to hear or see a single note of bitterness.

Dart knew about our work with children. He had, as long ago as 1959, written to us about our reported stages of development through which each child matures. Did we know, Dart wrote, "that they were almost exactly the stages of development which took place in the evolution of man?"

Dart's description of his struggle for acceptance made me think back over the past few years.

The question which brought us to Africa was, why do humans *have* to go through these stages? And what would happen if children were prevented from going through them on purpose? What about other countries? Do their children go through the same stages, and do they have the same or different kinds of reading problems? If our results were valid, we knew, they should apply anywhere in the world.

In an effort to gather as much information as possible, we visited England, France, and Italy, testing children with reading problems. We found them to be just like our American reading problems—they had not completely developed through the four stages and had the same neurological disorganization.

On one of our trips to Brazil, we stopped in the Republic of Panama to make a speech. It is unique, because right in the middle of it exists an American community, the Panama Canal Zone. Here there were different cultures living under the same geographical and climatic conditions. Testing some poor readers in Spanish-speaking Panama, we found that these children suffered the same lack in the development of their nervous systems as we had found with children in the United States and in Europe. Just across the street, in the Canal Zone, our American-born poor readers who now lived in Panama had the same deficiencies as did the Europeans, the Panamanians, and their fellow Americans.

We could see that geography or nationality had nothing to do with the problem. Reading problems could be traced to how the child had, or had not, developed his nervous system, regardless of where he lived.

Up to this point our testing had been done on comparatively similar cultures. Was it possible, we next asked, to find a culture so different from the European-American culture that, in effect, it didn't *allow* its children to develop their nervous systems? For instance, was there a culture somewhere in the world which didn't allow its children to crawl or creep? If we could find such people, we could learn more about what effect environment has on the development of nervous systems, since most of their children should fail our tests of development.

Glenn's airplane conversation began to plague us. Among primitive people at the equator there might be very few floors and, since the earth at the equator presents dangers to children from insects, poisonous plants, and snakes, mothers there would probably not allow a baby to crawl or creep. If we found a culture that drastically restricted its children in this way, what would their brain development be?

Through Veras, who was by this time the most renowned

rehabilitationist in all of Brazil, we were privileged to be invited by the Brazilian Government, through the *Fondacao Brasil Central*, to study their primitive Indians in the center of Brazil's Matte Grosso (Big Jungle). This area, south of the Amazon, contains the most primitive people on earth. It is deep equatorial rain forest, whose only routes of communication and travel are through the swollen rivers. The only entrance (from civilization) to this vast area is by small plane, flying north from the city of Brazilia, which was under construction at the time of our expeditions.

The single engine Cessna groaned as it could barely lift off the runway in Brazilia on our first expedition into the jungle, laden down with Veras, Glenn, Cidi the pilot, and myself. We learned a lot about each other on that first trip. Veras learned that Glenn and I each had a basic weakness, detrimental to this kind of activity—Glenn seemed to attract swarms of mosquitos, so Veras doubled the anti-malarial doses he administered to Glenn; I couldn't swim well, so each time we came to a swamp or a river, Veras swore in Portuguese and grabbed me by the arm and pulled me across the water. We were a strange threesome proceeding by river, on foot, or by plane through the jungle. Without the help of Claudio Villas Boas and his brother, Orlando Villas Boas, the legendary protectors of the Indians, we could not have succeeded. Sadly, the third brother, Leonardo, had died of a tropical disease just before our arrival. These men made available to us Indian tribes seldom, if ever, before seen by "civilizados."

As time went by, Cidi's hair-raising plane landings and take-offs in the open areas in the jungle became more routine and we all relaxed. Veras swore that he noticed fewer and fewer mosquitos surrounding Glenn and he assured me that my ability to cross streams improved daily.

The Indians exist in small tribes, living in villages usually found on natural clearings by a river; there is little, if any, communication between tribes. They are pre-stone age in culture;

they wear no clothing, don't use stone or metal, but have progressed to the point where they use wooden arrows with fish-bone tips. They are gatherers, not planters, living by fishing, some hunting, and the gathering of jungle fruit and roots. During four expeditions we visited tribes with such exotic names as Xingu, Caraja, Kalapalo, Chevanti, and Kamaiura. There were no floors in the large crude grass huts in which they lived.

We searched everywhere for babies on the ground—but could not find a single one. At each village we offered to pay mothers to place their up-to-eighteen month old babies on the ground, but they refused. We finally decided to force the issue with one tribe, so that we could photograph at least one creeping baby. We succeeded with a chief, who cajoled a mother into placing her one-year-old baby on the ground. The baby screamed with fright, the men of the village began to brandish their arrows, and the frightened mother snatched up her child and ran off into the jungle.

Our four expeditions into the interior of Brazil took place over a period of five years and never were we to see an Indian baby on the ground. We saw hundreds of babies, but they were always in the arms of mother, father, sister, or brother. When these babies reach the age of walking—we estimated this to be about two years of age, since they could not tell us because they had no number system—the parents simply place them on their feet and teach them to walk.

We tested many children of all ages for general neurological fitness and we found that, as a group, they were seriously lacking in nervous system development. We found that they had difficulty in using their two eyes together; their creeping was extremely awkward, and very few of the group had developed sidedness. They did not pass our tests for the development of the nervous system; in fact, most of them performed as poorly on our tests as did the European, Panamanian, and American children *with reading problems*. Interestingly, while each tribe had a crude spoken language, *none* of them had a written language.

These children could see well, because they shot birds out of trees, and fish under water with their bows and arrows, but they did not perceive as we do. Testing their ability to recognize symbols, we would place a fish on the ground and next to it we would draw a picture of a fish. They could see no relationship between the two. Their brains were unable to deal with the drawing of a fish as related to the actual fish. They certainly would not have been able to deal with any written code. It would be impossible to teach them to read, we knew, until they had developed the brain capacity to deal with symbols, which, of course, is written language. We theorized that the constant carrying of children had deprived them of the opportunity to crawl and creep, stunting the development of the nervous system. Since their brains were unable to deal with a code, they had never developed a written language.

And now we were here in Africa to see whether or not African tribal children were restricted in their development by custom. If they were, we predicted from our experiences in Brazil, they would have incomplete development of their nervous systems and would not have developed a written language. The Bushmen of the Kalahari Desert certainly duplicated what we had found in Brazil.

We all talked constantly throughout dinner until Marjorie interrupted, "Glenn and Carl, if you are getting an early start in the morning, we had better let you have some sleep."

We thought that was wise, because there were 4,500 miles of driving before we would reach Nairobi. We said goodnight and watched the Darts walk off, arm in arm. "Do you think he'll come to Philadelphia?" I whispered.

"I have an idea he will," Glenn responded. "He's too young, vital and excited to allow a new challenge just to lie there. Also, he's too curious about life and science not to pick it up and start a whole new career."

He was right.

Driving north we visited, lived with, and tested the children of many tribes, including the Bangwaketse and Batswana of Batswana, the Mashone and Matabele of west-central Rhodesia, the Lumwe and Yao of Southern Malawi, and Tonga of northern Malawi, the stately Masai of northern Tansania, and the Luo of the Lake Victoria district of Kenya.

None of these tribes, we quickly discovered, allow their babies to crawl or creep. Non-walking children are always carried on the mothers' backs. A blanket or shawl is ingeniously wrapped around the mother and tied in front. Baby is tucked in the blanket on his mother's back, with only his head sticking out of the wrapping, and he stares straight into the back of his mother's neck. Upon testing the development of the nervous systems of these children, we found they lacked development precisely as did the Brazilan Indian children. To us it was obvious that, here again, lack of opportunity, because of custom, had hindered development. Each tribe had a spoken language but none had a written language.

It became very obvious to us that if we took a newborn from one of the primitive tribes back with us to the United States and gave him every opportunity to develop his nervous system that he would not grow up as a primitive with no written language. Instead, he would think, act, and read as an American because of a more completely developed nervous system. Indeed, I became convinced that if one of my own children were transported to this region as a newborn, he would develop exactly like the tribal children.

We now had a mass of new evidence that *opportunity* for use was the key to the development of the nervous system. In order to develop properly, a child has to go through certain stages of brain development, ending in complete one-sidedness. If, for some reason, he is not allowed to go through a stage, whatever the restriction, a problem almost certainly will develop. These restrictions could range from a mother's constantly enveloping arms in the jungle of Brazil, to an ingeniously wrapped swaddling blanket in Africa, an igloo in the Arctic, or an attractively made restrictive playpen in the United States.

Back at the Institutes in Philadelphia we began to probe more deeply into American customs, looking for practices that tended to restrict the brain development of children who became reading problems.

Since eighty percent of American children developed normally, going through the necessary stages with no trouble and no help, we could not blame the inadequate development of the remaining twenty percent on cultural influences such as we had found in more primitive cultures. Checking our records for possibilities, we came up with a three-fold theory.

Our American reading problem existed in a four-to-one ratio of boys over girls. Although we didn't completely understand such a large difference, this ratio helped us to theorize about one of the causes. There was a small group in which the reading problems cropped up generation after generation, with the boys in the family having the problems, while the girls read rather well. This group tended to have left-handed or mixed-handed parents, and there were many more left-handers in this group than there were left-handers in the normal population. There were also many more instances of twins in these families than in the normal population. This small group, it appeared, had a genetic tendency toward mixed-handedness and, therefore, toward reading problems.

Another group seemed to be the result of environmental factors, such as early restrictions on creeping because of too much time in a playpen, or being kept too much in a walker, or the deliberate changing of handedness by a parent or teacher. (We were happy to note that, throughout the country, this environmental group is gradually diminishing as a result of greater knowledge about how children develop and how they should be reared.) The third group is generally classified through circumstantial evidence. These are children in whom we suspect but can't prove some mild injury to the brain. If we look at the history of a child in this group we might find a very difficult birth, perhaps times when he didn't receive enough oxygen, or ran very high temperatures, or had an accidental bump on the head. The usual neurological examination rarely picks up this kind of mild injury to the brain.

Perhaps this lack of development took place only in our European-based culture and with our left to right type of writing. Was this truly a world-wide problem? Glenn and I have looked at, studied, talked with, examined children in Brazil, Argentina, Peru, Morocco, Israel, Iran, Pakistan, India, Thailand, Malaysia, Indonesia, Fiji, and Russia. Their reading problems are just like ours; they lack complete nervous system development.

Race, color, religion, geography, or climate were not the answer. The opportunity given to the child to develop his nervous system was the answer.

Our studies had now helped us to locate causes. By taking careful histories of a child's family, birth, early development, illnesses, and accidents, we were able, more consistently, to pinpoint the cause of the reading problem; we could determine the stage at which the child had not sufficiently developed.

But the world was still going its merry way, using all the old techniques trying to solve reading problems, with a resounding lack of success. WHY wouldn't they listen? There was another group who chose to attack us, perhaps frightened by the specter of failure, which was increasingly made evident by the government, the press, television, and especially the parents.

Raymond and Marjorie Dart walked past my window. How could I be dejected when I saw that man? He had spent thirty years fighting to get the world to accept the truth. They came into my office and watched the usual, daily parade of children whose cases were exciting and invigorating.

Next door, Glenn was seeing another group of children. I could hear his laughter through the wall.

Each night after we had finished with the chidren, Glenn and I reviewed the day.

"Why so quiet, Carl?" he started that night.

"Glenn, it's October, it has been exactly seventeen years since we met. We've worked hard; we've helped thousands of children; we've both written a number of books on reading, all widely read; we've trained hundreds of students from all corners of the world, but still the world goes its merry way—either creating more reading problems without solving them, or occasionally attacking us for our attempts. Has that seventeen years of hard work been worth-while?"

Dart stood up, walked in his slightly bent fashion to the other side of the room and focused his penetrating blue eyes on us. We were slouched in our chairs in our shirt sleeves. I could sense that I had upset him and that Glenn and I were about to be lectured.

"I have learned a few things in my seventy-six years that I want to share with you,"—he paused.

"You must read the Proverbs to learn that knowledge is more precious then rubies. But knowledge is not enough, for it only initiates; understanding is more important.

"Both of you are being too hard on your detractors and too impatient with the world.

"Your detractors have some knowledge, but very little understanding. They have had understanding kept from them by their teachers and their culture. You must help them to understand.

"For the remainder of the world, which is not as upset as you are with these millions of reading problems, you must be patient. We know that until an action has taken place in man's evolution, he does not create the word for that action. Work on, create the action, then the world can give words to these actions and move on.

"At present the world you criticize is only becoming aware that there is a problem—let alone a solution."

His voice choked up as he continued:

"We all walk on the shoulders of our predecessors. Without Darwin I would be nothing. Without many people who preceded and taught you, you would be nothing. These past years have been glorious for both of you.

"Carl, I don't want to hear you ask that question in the future without your knowing the answer in your own heart."

I looked at Glenn sitting there. He looked older with his gray beard, but was still the same person who said originally, to me, "Welcome aboard." From the look on his face I knew he felt just the way I did. We were both reminded of the same uncomfortable feelings we had experienced sixteen years earlier when we had sat on J. B. Priestley's chairs at Fay's.

Chapter 8

THERAPY AT HOME

THE SEARCH had taken seventeen long years. It had never been easy or comfortable, but it was always exciting. I was periodically shattered by failure, I was often discouraged by the criticism that any new idea draws, but each success brought new hope and enthusiasm. I had learned many lessons from brain-injured children, and I was learning to apply those lessons to reading problem children.

To be of real value, a system of solving reading problems also had to be practical. A child who lives with a reading problem for a long time, understandably, quite often develops some psychological problems. Spending too long working at solving the problem often further discourages an already discouraged child. Going to institutions, schools, or tutors, daily or weekly, presents problems of discouragement, practicability, and cost.

We had to devise a program that would not add to the child's frustration and was practical in terms of time required and family funds available. Faced with these requirements, we devised a home program that could be supervised by the child's parents.

Under our new system we diagnosed the child on his first visit. We tested him thoroughly, took a lengthy history from both parents, and evaluated the child to see how he performed at each stage of development. We then taught both the child and his parents how to go back to the lowest stage at which he had failed a developmental test. At home, the child followed a careful program of daily therapy under the supervision of his parents. Since the child and parents were executing the program, we found it necessary and helpful to explain the theory and the problem in great detail to both parents and child.

At approximately two-month intervals the child and his parents returned for re-evaluation. The child was given tests and his development was re-evaluated. In addition, a history was taken and school reports reviewed. Following this, the child returned home, and he and his parents undertook a revised program, based on his needs and progress, for another two-month period.

The children we began to see ranged in age from 8 to 16. They seemed normal in every way except that they had reading problems. Because the theory was so new and so different we saw, for the most part, children who had already been through many of the more usual treatment procedures, without success. Few came to us who had not had one or more of the standard remedial techniques used on them, such as psychiatry, psychological counseling, tutoring, phonetics, tracing, or repeating one or more grades. Whatever had been done for these children had failed, since they continued to have reading problems and were still having trouble at school. For most of these children we seemed to represent the last hope.

We decided that we could treat about 200 new children with reading problems per year. Since each child returned for re-evaluation visits every two months, we had to plan to see each child a minimum of 6 visits per year until he was discharged.

We discharged children when we were satisfied with their reading progress and when we became convinced that they could survive at school and could continue to improve their reading along with their classmates. In 1965 we discharged 63 children; in 1966 we discharged 60; in 1967 we discharged 67; and in 1968 we discharged 60. The group discharged in 1965 had required an average of 4.5 re-evaluation visits; the group discharged in 1966 required an average of 5.2 re-evaluation visits; the group discharged in 1967 required an average of 4.9 re-evaluation visits; and the group discharged in 1968 required an average of 4.9 re-evaluation visits.

However, to look at only those who had improved enough to be discharged is misleading. To be more practical, one must ask, "What is the average rate of improvement made by a more random group over a set period of treatment?"

Recently we pulled at random from our files the records of 185 children with reading problems. They had carried out a program at home under their parents' supervision for at least six months. We compared their original standardized test scores in reading with those made six months later. These children ranged in age from 8 to 16; there were 134 boys and 51 girls, and they had varying severity of reading problems. All of them had two things in common: they all seemed normal, except that they had reading problems, and before coming to us they all had received some form of therapy or remedial training, which had not solved their problems.

The average reading progress for children who do not have reading problems is one-half a school year, or six months of growth for each six months of elapsed time. A child with a reading problem has obviously not developed at this rate of speed; he has obviously made less than six months' progress in reading for each six-month elapsed period, and, as a result, has fallen behind.

The average gain made by our random group of 185 children was 8.3 months during the *six-month* period of home treatment. This group was not only making normal growth but had exceeded the *normal* rate of development during the *six-month* period by 2.3 months, while carrying out the program at home under the supervision of their parents. The progress made by individual children in this group ranged from no progress to over four years during the six-month period. (See Chart I of the Appendix.)

In order to learn more about the average rate of progress, we studied a group of fifty consecutive new children who came to the Institutes for treatment. Their average age at the time they first came to us was 9½ years, varying from 8 to 16. These were normal children in regular schools who had severe reading problems. They also had been treated by one or more other methods, which had failed, before they came to us.

They were treated at home by their parents for an average of *4.6 months*. A normal reader would be expected to make *4.6 months'* progress during this period. This group made an average of 7.1 months' progress. They not only made a normal rate of progress during the 4.6 months of treatment, but they exceeded the normal rate by 2.5 months. (See Chart 2 of the Appendix.)

It had taken time, but we now had answers. Most reading problems were the result of some lack of development in a child's nervous system. Through testing, we could find at which stage of brain development the child was inadequate. We had also learned that brain development *could* be changed. We had to give the child the opportunity to relive the stage which he had somehow skipped or had not completed. Fortunately we found that when parents and children understood the program and what they were to do, the program could be carried out successfully at home.

THE TREATMENT
OF READING PROBLEMS

Chapter 9

HOW TO USE PART TWO

THIS SECTION, CONSISTING of seven chapters, provides you with a complete program for treating your child's reading problem at home. It is the program that has proved successful not only at the Institutes for the Achievement of Human Potential, but in schools and colleges throughout the country, as well as in many other Institutes founded on its methods. While by no means too difficult for the lay person to grasp, this written presentation does require some initial close attention to gain a clear understanding of the progressive steps—obviously, the better you understand what you are doing, the smoother will the program run and the more successful will be its outcome.

Perhaps the best approach is this: read steadily through the seven chapters in order to get their drift and feel, putting a pencil mark against whatever is not immediately clear. Then re-read the chapters, again straight through, but this time stopping at the marked portions for as long as necessary. It would be a good idea, where special physical tests are described, to perform some of these on yourself first, so that you can apply them to your child with confidence.

But first, how do you know your child has a reading problem? Most parents are told, others find out on their own.

The day your child went off to school for the first time is a day to be remembered. But much harder to forget is the day you were told, "Your child has a reading problem." Most often, for both parent and child, this is the beginning of long years of frustration and worry.

It may have happened in late spring of the kindergarten year. Perhaps you arrived for a conference with the teacher, who discussed "reading readiness," a subject in which your child had scored badly. If you were not too surprised to ask questions, you inquired what a low score in that subject meant, and were told, "He isn't mature enough to go into the first grade, *where we teach reading,* and he should repeat kindergarten to gain the necessary maturity." In essence, he wasn't old enough or grown up enough to learn to read.

If you missed that danger signal, the next opportunity for informing parents of a child's disability usually comes in February of the first-grade year. This is often done by letter: "Bobby is having difficulty mastering the required sight vocabulary at the pre-primer level. Would you please review this vocabulary so that he can master the list at the back of the book? We can then move on to the primer level." Frequently, despite all the help he gets at home, Bobby never does master the sight vocabulary, and another family takes on the burden of a child who can't read.

Perhaps your child made it to the second grade without being tabbed. Then you may have received something like the following: "Bobby has a good sight vocabulary in reading. Up to this point he has not mastered beginning and ending consonants, and his word attack skill and phonetic ability are weak. Would you please review the enclosed phonetic cards with him?" Much more ominous is getting the bad news at the third-grade level, when you, yourself, suspect that Bobby does not read as well as he should. This is usually a cryptic request to attend a conference with Bobby's teacher, ending, "Oh, by the way, the principal will be there and you might bring your husband along." At this meeting, if some puzzled parent ventured to ask how Bobby had been taught, he would hear that the school was "eclectic" and Bobby had been taught by *all* methods.

Then came the inevitable appointment with the child psychologist for "tests" which, as you were told by the principal, were to be given to find the "underlying factors in your child's reading problem." As a rule, these include an intelligence test, to see if he is bright enough to be able to learn to read. If, after one of these tests, you happened to watch a three-year-old blithely reading all the labels in the supermarket, you might well begin to wonder: "Just how stupid do they think my child is?"

Usually, the intelligence tests result in the discovery that the child is normal, and you are advised, incidentally, not to set your educational sights too high. Following this, you may also have been offered some comfort with the information that the school your child attends is above average, so that the level of competition is intense. Next came the *projective* or *personality* part of the tests. The theory behind this is "Does the child want to read?" or perhaps "Is he punishing someone by not reading?" Here from our files, is a sample report of such a test:

"A study was made of Bobby's personality adjustments. These materials indicate him to be a masculinely oriented youngster with a positive conscience, and thus, the intention and desire to conform and achieve. There is much in the way of shifting orientation with respect to emotional needs, indecision, and inability contributing to his turmoil. The emotional stress tends to produce feelings of inadequacy and inferiority in Bobby, feelings that are aided and abetted by his actual lack of successful achievement. His ego, therefore, is not strong and does not provide him with any strength in organizing capacity. His emotional control tends to be fluctuating and there is seen here the inclination to accumulate a great deal of diffuse anxiety and tension, which, in turn, would also interfere with attention and sustaining concentration."

All of which means that the child can't read because he is not praised or rewarded enough when he does—which usually leaves matters just about where they were, since, as most parents have found, rewards and praise don't really seem to help much.

If you live in a metropolitan area you may have gone to a "reading clinic," where the tests become a two- or three-day affair, followed by a report something like this:

"We administered twenty-four tests to Bobby. They included a reading inventory, mastery of initial and ending consonants, mastery of vowels, phonetic and structural word attack skills, speed of reading and comprehension. You can see from the enclosed profile that Bobby is poor in all these areas, only reaching the eighth percentile for his age norm. His reading frustration level is two years behind that of his grade level."

In short, he can't read. You may have reacted by saying, "You don't have to tell me he can't read. I told you that three days ago. That's why I brought him here in the first place. What shall I *do* about it?" You were then referred to the recommendation portion of the report which advised "added practice in the form of individual tutoring with a trained remedial specialist who will keep in mind his low frustration level."

But the tutoring, as it usually turns out, fails to achieve any great change.

The reading clinic may also have given your child's problem an impressive technical name such as *strephosymbolia, alexia, dyslexia, specific dyslexia,* or *word blindness,* which perhaps prompted you to believe that your child's special problem had been isolated and was, therefore, on the way to being cured. Unfortunately, these names have not provided much help in the search for solutions. Translated, they *all* simply mean the child can't read.

But you may never have been told officially that your child had a reading problem. There still remain a few schools—gradually disappearing, which have a complete hands-off policy. In fact, these schools never seem to say anything about reading in their report cards. They really do not believe in conferences. They wait until the sixth grade or above, until the month of

June and then, attached to the final report, you find this shocker: "We are sorry to inform you that Bobby will be retained in sixth grade. His reading scores on our recent achievement tests do not qualify him to go on to the Junior High School."

There are many children who read just well enough to survive at school. These are the children who struggle with the reading that the school requires but never read an additional word because reading is such a struggle.

If your child is any of these children and if you feel that he has a reading problem, follow the instructions in Chapters 10 and 11 for evaluation, that is, for determining the level of development at which your child may be deficient. In these there are questions to be answered in which you must call on your special knowledge of your child as well as some simple physical tests. Together, these two methods of evaluation will reveal, will pinpoint, the *stage* of development that calls for therapy. Succeeding chapters describe in detail the program to be carried out for each particular stage indicated.

Before beginning any treatment discuss it fully and openly with your child; his willing cooperation is essential. And praise him as he progresses. Whether your child is 6 or 16 he will enjoy and be stimulated by praise and sympathetic encouragement.

Chapter 10

CHECKING YOUR CHILD'S HISTORY

THE FIRST INQUIRY concerns your child's family background, and will help determine whether the problem may be inherited. A small percentage of reading problems, we have found, does indeed run in families. Happily, however, they respond to treatment in the same manner as the others.

Write your answers to the following questions, each of which may be answered by a *yes* or a *no*, in the space provided. *All no answers will be discarded as not significant; all yes answers indicate a possible area of difficulty.*

Answer *yes* or *no*:

1. Is either mother or father left-handed or ambidextrous? _____

2. Are any of his brothers or sisters, over the age of six, left-handed or ambidextrous? _____

3. Were any of his grandparents left-handed or ambidextrous? _____

4. Are there reading problems among his aunts, uncles, or cousins? _____

5. Are there other reading problems in the immediate family, that is, parents, brothers, or sisters? _____

If you have any *yes* answers to these questions, there is a possibility that your child's problem is of a familial type. This makes no difference in either diagnosis or treatment. We have found, however, that children with familial type problems need a bit more time in treatment for establishing complete one-sidedness.

PREGNANCY AND BIRTH

A critical time in the development of a nervous system is the period of pregnancy, labor, and birth. The following analysis will provide assurance of your child's having a perfectly conditioned brain at the beginning, or it may indicate that his otherwise normal brain suffered some slight shock that resulted in a slowing down of the development of the whole nervous system. A prolonged labor, for instance (over 18 hours), or too short (under 2 hours), sometimes makes it difficult for the newborn's brain cells to get enough oxygen at the right time. Some cells, as a result, may suffer mild shock and, therefore, not begin their functions when they should. In extreme cases, some of the brain cells may have suffered extreme shock, or such a loss of oxygen, that they have not been able to function at all.

This is not as serious as it once was thought. The human brain consists of so many cells that the loss of a few, or the lack of function in a few, is no longer considered hopeless. The important question is what the child does with the billions of *remaining* healthy brain cells.

1. Was there any difficulty in maintaining the pregnancy? _____

2. Were there any illnesses or high temperatures during pregnancy? _____

3. Were there any accidents during pregnancy? _____

4. Was the duration of the pregnancy different in any way? Was it less than 270 or more than 290 days? _____

5. Was mother taking any special medications during pregnancy? _____

6. Was the labor either very long or very short—less than two or more than eighteen hours? _____

7. Was the birth delayed for any reason?   _____

8. Were instruments used to aid in the birth?   _____

9. Was there a delay of more than a minute in the birth cry?   _____

10. Was the baby's color abnormal in any way when you first saw him?   _____

11. Did the doctor who first examined your child tell you that anything was wrong wth him?   _____

You have now checked on your child's heredity, as it relates to reading, and his gestation period as well as the labor and birth process. If you have all "no" answers, the probability is that none of these is related to your child's reading problem. Now we must check your child's development from *birth to six months* of age. Answer *yes* or *no*.

STAGE 1.   *Birth to Six Months of Age*

1. Did he have trouble eating or sleeping?   _____

2. Did he cry more than usual?   _____

3. Did he have high fevers with temperatures over 100°?   _____

4. Did he seem too sluggish to you?   _____

5. Did he seem too active to you?   _____

6. Did he have trouble recognizing members of the family?   _____

7. Was he exceptionally upset by loud sounds?   _____

If you have pictures of your child taken during the birth to six months period, they will help you to answer the next questions:

1. Was there anything different or strange about the movement of his arms, legs, or body?   _____

2. Did he use one side of his body better than the other?   _____

3. Did his eyes look strange in any way, such as being of different sizes or having a deviation of one eye?   _____

STAGE 2. *Six Months to One Year of Age*

Answer *yes* or *no*. Again, you will find pictures, if available, quite helpful in refreshing your memory.

1. Did he have any prolonged (over two days) high temperatures (over 100°) during this time? _____

2. Was he in a playpen on an average of more than two hours a day? _____

3. Did he lack curiosity when placed on the floor? _____

4. Was he put in a walker, on an average, for more than one hour per day? _____

5. Did he ever consistently roll over or slide on his seat in getting from place to place? _____

6. Were his two eyes different in size from each other? _____

7. Did either eye ever "wander"?

8. Did he creep in any way other than in cross-pattern? _____

STAGE 3. *One to Two Years of Age*

1. Did he walk early (under ten months)? _____

2. Did he walk late (over eighteen months)? _____

3. Did he have more than the usual number of falls when compared to other children of the same age? _____

4. Did his beginning speech seem abnormal to you in any way? _____

5. Did he have trouble understanding you when you talked to him? _____

6. Did he have trouble feeding himself? _____

7. Did he seem overly active? _____

8. Did he seem sluggish? _____

9. Did he have trouble learning the few rules which you taught him? _____

10. Did his eyes ever cross or wander after he started to walk? _____

11. Did he have trouble with his balance after he had been walking for over four months? _____

12. Did you ever think he was hard of hearing? _____

The next set of questions reviews his entire developmental history, up to the present time. Answer *yes* or *no*.

1. Did he ever have a head injury? _____

2. Was he ever knocked unconscious? _____

3. Did he ever have trouble with his hearing? _____

4. Did he ever have trouble with his vision? _____

5. Did either eye ever turn in or out when he was tired? _____

6. Were you ever concerned about his poor coordination? _____

7. Did he ever go through a stage of falling frequently, other than in beginning walking? _____

8. Did he ever have any severe injuries? _____

9. Did he ever have any severe illnesses? _____

10. Were you ever concerned about his poor speech? _____

If you have all *no* answers, you can assume that your child's nervous system was reasonably intact at birth and that there seemed to be no accidents which might have harmed it during the first few years of life. If you have any *yes* answers at any stage, you can begin to suspect that a developmental lag may exist at that stage. You will be able to check on this in the next chapter, as you evaluate your child's actual physical performance at each stage.

At this point, you must talk to your child's reading teacher, preferably at school where her records are available. The purpose is to prepare a small file on your child so that you may make a more accurate judgment as to his progress during the therapy program. Ask the teacher the following questions, making a note of her answers.

1. What are her opinions, generally, about your child's reading, writing, and spelling? Any *particular* kinds of spelling errors?

2. What is the child's actual grade level in reading? The grade level is given in years and months. As an example, a child whose grade level is 2.5 reads as well as the average child who is in the fifth month of the second grade. A child who reads at 4.0 reads as well as the average child who is in the beginning of the fourth grade.

3. Does he do everything right-handed? Left-handed? Is he ambidextrous?

4. Does his general physical coordination compare well with that of the other children?

5. Is he happy at school? Does he get on well with other children or does he seem to feel defeated by an inability to compete?

6. Does the child ever "reverse" in his reading or writing? That is, does he read, or write, whole words or parts of words backward, such as "was" for "saw" or 24 for 42?

7. Ask for a sample of his handwriting done at school.

8. Ask for suggestions as to how you can be of help with your child at home.

Following this conference with the teacher, consult your notes and write out what you learned about the child, using this outline:

1. Grade level score.
2. Spelling errors.
3. Handwriting.
4. Interest in reading.
5. Suggestions.
6. Reversals.
7. Handedness.
8. Coordination.

If during the conference, the teacher feels that your child is presently making good progress in reading, *don't begin this program*. Instead, follow the teacher's suggestions and set up another appointment in two months. At that time you can compare your child's two reading scores to see if he *is* making good progress.

You now have a history of each stage of your child's development. You have some ideas as to the condition of his nervous system at birth, and some possible reasons for a lack of complete development. You also have learned from his teacher exactly where he stands in reading at the present time and you have started a file so that you can keep a record of his progress. Now you are ready to test your child physically at each developmental stage to see what his actual performance may indicate.

Chapter 11

EVALUATING
YOUR CHILD'S DEVELOPMENT

HAVING GONE over your child's developmental history, you have arrived at some tentative conclusions as to the levels at which he did or did not perform well. You can check these *possible* areas of interference by giving him some physical tests to see how he performs *now* at each of these levels.

Start by checking him at the lowest stage of development, then move on to successively higher stages. As you complete each stage, be sure to record whether your child passes or fails.

These tests are applicable for children from six to sixteen. It is possible to check on these stages *now* because of the brain's tendency to accumulate and store experiences. Even though the brain has little, if any, use for a function, once learned, it is retained. These "vestigial" (stored but unused) functions are retained by the brain as a form of insurance. In the event that higher functions ever deteriorate or are injured and don't function, these old and unused patterns can come to the fore and take over. As a result of the brain's tendency to serve as a storehouse for all that has happened to it, these functions can be brought out and tested; hence, we can test a child's creeping, even though he has been walking for years.

STAGE 1. *The Birth to Six Month Age of Alternate One-Sidedness*

A—Sleep Pattern

Checking your child's crawling ability is difficult because sliding along a floor creates friction between his clothes and the floor, making it difficult to move smoothly. In our studies we found a relationship between how a child crawls and the position in which he sleeps, so we can test this while your child is asleep.

Explain to your child that you are going to observe him while he is asleep and that the observation requires that he sleep on his stomach. If he does not naturally sleep on his stomach, have him practice so that he will become comfortable doing so. When he has adjusted to sleeping in this manner, occasionally step in his room while he is asleep and observe the position in which he sleeps. Ideally he should sleep in a left-sided or a right-sided position. See Photos 1 and 2.

If he sleeps in *either* of these positions on four successive observations, he passes the test at this level. We accept either the left-sided or right-sided position for passing this test because we all naturally change our positions a few times each hour while asleep. The child who is well developed at this stage usually moves from one of these positions to the other throughout the night.

If you do not find him in either of these positions in four consecutive observations, try this test. While he is asleep on his stomach, take his head gently in your hands and turn it in the opposite direction from where you find it. If he allows you to turn his head and does not change his body position as a reaction, or if he allows you to turn his head and does not return it to its original position, or if he allows you to turn his head and doesn't awaken, he *fails* this test.

If when you turn his head his body position changes, or if

when you turn his head he turns it back to where it was, or if when you turn his head he awakens, he *passes* at this level.

Try this test once each night for four successive nights. Remember, if he allows you to turn his head while he is asleep with no reaction (moving his body, turning his head back, or waking) he fails at this level.

	Pass	Fail
	_____	_____

B—*Visual Pursuit*

You will recall that alternate one-sidedness is typical of this stage. The visual test at this stage is aimed at seeing whether your child can follow smoothly his right hand with his right eye and his left hand with his left eye. If your child wears glasses, have him wear them for this test. Have him cover his left eye with his left hand. Have him hold an object in his right hand at arm's length. Have him move it up and down, horizontally, in a circle, and up and down at an angle, following it with his right eye. Watch his right eye. Does it follow the hand smoothly? Are the eye movements jerky? Does he overshoot the target?

Now, do the same for the left eye and hand while he covers the right eye. If either eye follows the object in a start-and-stop fashion, doesn't follow it at all, or doesn't follow it smoothly, he *fails* this test. If he follows each hand smoothly with each eye in every direction, he *passes* the test.

You can now record whether he has passed the sleep pattern and the visual tests at Stage 1, or has failed them. Record "pass" or "fail":

	Pass	Fail
A—Sleep pattern	_____	_____
B—Visual pursuit	_____	_____

STAGE 2. *The Six-Month to One-Year Level Typified by Two-Sidedness*

A—*Cross-Pattern Creeping*

Ask your child to creep on his hands and knees. Use the largest room in your house that has a rug. Your child's age will make little difference in how he performs; his previous experience at this stage and his development will make the difference. Watch him closely as he creeps. His creeping should be smooth and rhythmical. It must be in cross-pattern, that is, the right hand and left knee should strike the floor simultaneously. Then the left hand and right knee should strike the floor simultaneously. The hands should be palm down and flat and the fingers should point forward. Since the opposite hand and knee are being used simultaneously, the balance and the rhythm should be smooth and natural. See Photos 3, 4, and 5.

If you have any questions as to what constitutes good cross-pattern creeping, there is a very easy way to learn about it. Watch a nine-month-old, who has not been kept in a playpen, creep. You will see that his creeping is quite smooth and rhythmical, even though the baby gives no thought to the creeping motions. Watch to see how the opposite hand and knee are automatically synchronized. Although your child has not crept for a long time, he should still retain the pattern. It will not be as gracefully done as the nine-month-old's creeping, but the *pattern* should be the same.

In order to pass this test your child must do all the following:

1. Creep in the proper cross-pattern.
2. Creep with his knees at least eight inches apart.
3. Creep with a smooth rhythm.
4. Creep with his hands and fingers flat and pointing forward.
5. Creep with his feet dragging along the floor.

If these are not done correctly, he *fails* this test.

                                        Pass   Fail

                                   _____   _____

B—*Vision*

The next test is aimed at finding whether he uses his two eyes together. Try it on yourself first.

Look into a mirror with the mirror light on. Look at one of your eyes in the mirror. You will notice a small pinpoint of light that is a reflection of the light hitting your wet and reflecting eyeball. Move your head so that the pinpoint of light hits your eye just at the edge of the pupil. Now look at your other eye. The pinpoint of light should appear in both eyes at about the same relation to both pupils. When we see this in children, we call them bright-eyed. It really means that they use their two eyes together well.

Now look at your child's eyes. If he wears glasses, do this *without* them. Do you see a reflection of the light in both eyes? Does the pin-point of light strike the two eyes at the same place in relation to the pupil?

If the answers to these two questions are *yes*, he passes this test; if not, he *fails*.

                                        Pass   Fail

                                   _____   _____

C—*Visual Pursuit*

You can now further test his visual performance at this stage by giving him an object to hold in *his* hand at arm's length. Have him move the object—it can be a pencil, small flashlight, or anything to which he will pay attention—in all directions. Have him make a full circle with it, move it straight up and down, sideways, and at various up and down angles. If your child wears glasses, have him wear them for this test. Ask him to follow, with *both eyes*, the object which is in his hand. Watch his eyes. They should follow the object in his hand smoothly and without jerky start-and-stop motion. If the eyes follow the object in a start-and-stop manner, or if they don't follow at all, or if only one eye follows, your child *fails* this test. If both eyes follow his hand smoothly in all directions, he *passes* the test. Record your answers for Stage 2.

		Pass	Fail
A.	Creeping (cross-pattern)	_____	_____
B.	Vision	_____	_____
C.	Visual Pursuit	_____	_____

STAGE 3. *The Twelve- to Eighteen-Month-Old Level of Development*

A—*Cross-Pattern Walking*

The first test in Stage 3 is cross-pattern walking. In normal walking the *opposite* hand and foot move forward at the same time. This gives added balance to man's walking. No other creature walks in this manner. As the *right foot* moves forward in taking a step, the *left hand* moves forward, serving as a counterbalance to the foot. As the *left foot* moves forward the *right hand* moves forward. To get a better understanding of normal walking, stand on a sidewalk and watch people walking toward you. You will notice that most of them walk in cross-pattern. Now watch them from the side. You can now see the rhythm involved in cross-pattern walking, which is normal human walking. See Photos 6 and 7.

Now *you* practice cross-pattern walking. Make it deliberate and slightly exaggerated normal walking, so that you will be able to demonstrate it to your child for the test. After you have practiced, you are ready to give the test. The test is done as follows: Say to your child, "Watch me walk. Notice that I am pointing with my finger to the opposite (different) foot as I walk." Now demonstrate for eight or nine steps.

1. Right-sided sleep pattern; see page 104. Same as crawling pattern; see page 124.

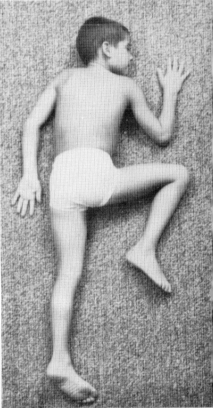

2. Left-sided sleep pattern; see page 104. Same as crawling pattern; see page 124.

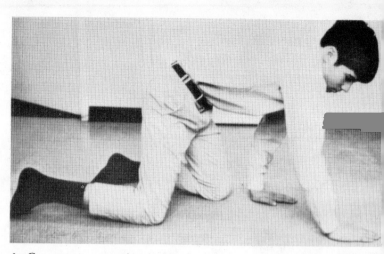

3. Cross-pattern creeping; see page 110.

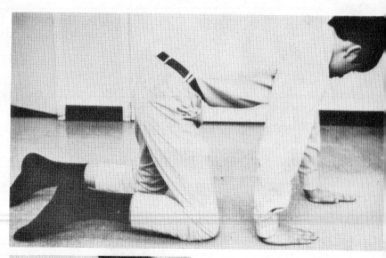

4. Cross-pattern creeping; see page 110.

5. Cross-pattern creeping; see page 110.

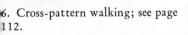

6. Cross-pattern walking; see page 112.

7. Cross-pattern walking; see page 112.

8. Eyedness: Far-point sighting (both eyes at a distance); see page 117.

9. Eyedness: Near-point sighting (near vision); see page 118.

10. Writing position: Head and paper positioning; see page 119.

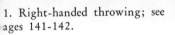

11. Right-handed throwing; see pages 141-142.

12. Right-handed throwing; see pages 141-142.

13. Right-handed throwing; see pages 141-142.

14. Left-handed throwing; see pages
141-142.

15. Left-handed throwing; see pages
141-142.

16. Left-handed throwing; see pages 141-142.

Now say to your child, "I want you to do what I do. Walk for me like this, pointing to the opposite (different) foot as you walk." Now demonstrate again for eight or nine steps. Then say, "Now you do it."

Watch him as he walks. Watch to see that the opposite arm and leg move at the same time. The rhythm should be smooth and the walking should be graceful. Your child *fails* this test if he does any of the following:

1. Walks with wrong rhythm or wrong pattern.
2. Walks using the arm and leg on the same side of the body at the same time.
3. Crosses the feet while walking.
4. Walks with obvious lack of balance.
5. Goes through much starting and stopping before he gets started.

He *passes* the test if he walks in a smooth cross-pattern. Record as *pass* or *fail*.

Pass	Fail
_____	_____

B—*Running*

Now take your child outdoors and ask him to run for you on a flat open area. Watch to see whether the cross-pattern motion is typical of his running. Is his running smooth and graceful? If it is not, he is probably not using both his arms and legs in rhythm to help him. Your child *passes* the running test if he runs in a smooth and graceful cross-pattern, pumping alternate arms as he runs. If his arms are not used in a cross-pattern rhythm, if they hang by his side, or if they are waved about haphazardly as he runs, he *fails* this test.

Pass	Fail
_____	_____

C—*Visual Pursuit*

If your child normally wears glasses, have him wear them for this test. The first test of vision at this stage is having him follow with *both* eyes an object held in *your* hand. Hold the object about twenty-four inches away from his eyes. Slowly move it in a circle, straight up and down, horizontally and up and down at an angle. If he follows the object in a start-and-stop fashion, or if he has difficulty following, he *fails* this test. If he follows the object in your hand with both of his eyes smoothly, he *passes* this test.

You will notice that his following the object in *your* hand can be very different from following the object in *his* hand. These represent two different levels of brain development; following your hand is more difficult than following his own hand. He could be good at one and poor at the other. Record *pass* or *fail* for this test.

                                        Pass   Fail

                                    _____   _____

D—*Head-Paper Distance*

Next, ask him to sit at his desk. Ask him to make a fist. With a tape measure, measure the distance between his elbow and the beginning of his fist at the first knuckle. Remember this distance. Now ask him to write his name and address while still seated at the desk. If he cannot write, ask him to crayon a picture. While he is writing or crayoning, measure the distance between his eyes and the paper. Is it within two inches of the distance which you measured as the distance between his elbow and his first knuckle? If it is, he *passes* this test of head-paper distance. If his face is *more* than two inches closer, or *more* than two inches farther from the paper than the elbow-to-knuckle measurement which you made, he *fails* this test. Now record his *pass* or *fail* marks for this stage:

	Pass	Fail
A. Walking (cross-pattern)	———	———
B. Running	———	———
C. Visual Pursuit	———	———
D. Head-Paper Distance	———	———

STAGE 4. *The Eighteen-Month to Six-Year Stage of Developing Complete One-Sidedness*

All tests in this stage are evaluated and recorded as *right, left,* or *mixed.*

A—*Handedness*

Start by observing his handedness. Does he do everything right-handed or left-handed, or does he alternate? Ask him to do the following tasks and record your observation. Wait a few hours and then test him again. These activities must *always* be done with the *right* hand if you are to record it as *right.* They must *always* be done with the *left* hand if you are to record it as *left.* If your child makes use of the opposite hand on any try, you must record the test as *mixed.*

Ask him to do the following:

	HANDEDNESS		
	Right	*Left*	*Mixed*
1. Write or crayon	———	———	———
2. Eat	———	———	———
3. Throw a ball	———	———	———
4. Pick up objects	———	———	———
5. Brush his teeth	———	———	———
6. Pound with a hammer	———	———	———
7. Cut with scissors	———	———	———
8. Throw darts	———	———	———

These tests are to be repeated on three separate occasions, at least four hours apart. Remember that to be marked *right* on a single test, such as writing, he must use the *right* hand exclusively on every one of the three tries; to be marked *left* he must use the *left* hand exclusively on every one of the three tries; otherwise, he is marked *mixed*.

Record your answers after the third repetition of these tests. Record each one as *right*, *left*, or *mixed*.

B—*Footedness*

Now test him for footedness. Ask him to do the following on three different testings, then put a check mark in the proper column.

	FOOTEDNESS		
	Right	*Left*	*Mixed*
1. Kick a stationary ball of any size.	_____	_____	_____
2. Place some marbles on the floor and have him pick them up with his bare toes. Which foot is more accurate?	_____	_____	_____
Which foot is faster?	_____	_____	_____
3. While he is barefoot, have him try to write his name with each foot. He should hold the pencil between his toes. If he has trouble with a pencil, try a large crayon. Which is better written?	_____	_____	_____

On all three testings he must complete each test with his right foot *exclusively* to be recorded as right; he must complete each test with his left foot *exclusively* to be recorded as left; otherwise, record him as mixed.

C—*Eyedness*

1. *Both Eyes at Distance*

If your child normally wears glasses, have him wear them for *all* these tests of eyedness.

Roll up a sheet of paper into a tube. Wrap a rubber band around it so that it stays rolled up. Hand the tube to your child and ask him to look through it while holding it at arm's length in two hands—as he would a telescope. *Be sure he keeps both eyes open.* Have him look out a window and ask him to sight at a specific target through the tube. Now ask him to bring the tube back to his eyes slowly *without losing sight of the target.* Notice to which eye he brings the tube. Take the tube, choose another target and once again hand him the tube. Ask him to look at the target through the tube, at arm's length, holding it with both hands. *Remember, he is to keep both eyes open.* Ask him to bring the tube back to his eyes slowly and without losing the target. Record the eye to which he brings the tube. Do it once more.

To be recorded as *right* he should bring the tube back to his *right* eye on all three tests; to be recorded *left* he must bring the tube back to his *left* eye on all three tests; otherwise, he is recorded as *mixed.*

Right	*Left*	*Mixed*

2. *One Eye at Distance*

Take a sheet of paper and make a hole through the center of it with a pencil point. Have your child hold the piece of paper in both hands so that he can *see through* the hole in the center of the sheet of paper. Ask him to hold the paper at arm's length away from his face.

Now ask him to look out a window. Choose a specific target for him to sight with *both* eyes open while looking through the hole in the paper. Ask him to bring the paper back to his face slowly without losing sight of the target. Notice to which eye he brings the hole in the paper. *Do this three times.*

If he brings the hole in the paper to his *right* eye three times out of three, record this test as *right;* if he brings it to his *left* eye three times out of three, record this test as left; otherwise, record it as *mixed.*

	Right	Left	Mixed
	_____	_____	_____

3. *Near Vision*

Have your child sit at a desk. Make another tube from a sheet of paper. This time be sure that the tube is only four inches long. Place a piece of paper on the desk in front of your child. With a pencil make a small x in the middle of the paper.

Hand your child the tube and ask him to hold it with both hands. Now ask him to look through the tube at the x and to keep *both* eyes open. When he sights the x, ask him to bring the tube back to his face slowly and without losing sight of the x. Record the eye to which he brings the tube. Do this three times.

To be recorded on this test as *right* your child must bring the tube back to his *right* eye three times in three tries; to be recorded as *left,* he must bring it back to his *left* eye three times out of three; otherwise, record it as *mixed.*

	Right	Left	Mixed
	_____	_____	_____

4. *Near Vision With One Eye*

In the middle of a 3″ x 5″ card make a hole no larger than ¼ inch in diameter. A pencil point will make an adequately sized hole. While your child is still seated at the desk with the sheet of paper with a small x on it in front of him, hand him this card. Ask him to look at the x through the small hole in the card, with both eyes open. Then ask him to bring the card slowly back to his face without losing sight of the x. Record to which eye he brings the card. Do this test three times.

To be recorded as *right* he must bring the card to his *right* eye three times out of three tries; to be recorded *left*, he must bring it to his *left* eye three times out of three; otherwise, record it as *mixed*.

Right	*Left*	*Mixed*
_____	_____	_____

5. *Writing Position*

Now ask your child, who is still seated at his desk, to write his name, or to crayon if he cannot write. Watch him as he writes. Watch his head position. Notice if he moves his head from side to side as he writes. If he does, he is making constant visual adjustments and needs help in developing a dominant eye.

Now stand in front of him as he writes. If he is right-handed his face should be slightly rotated toward his left and his head should be tilted slightly toward his left, placing the right eye in the best position for seeing. If he is left-handed his face should be turned slightly toward his right and his head should be tilted slightly toward his right, placing his left eye in the best position for seeing. See Photo 10.

If your child's head position for writing is right, record this test as *right*; if it is *left*, record this test as *left*; if it is neither, or if he moves his head as he writes, record it as *mixed*.

Right	*Left*	*Mixed*
_____	_____	_____

6. *Paper Angle*

Seat your child at a desk and ask him to write for you. Look at the angle of the paper as it relates to the angle of the forearm of his writing hand. The paper and the forearm should be parallel to each other. A right-hander with proper paper angle will have a paper angle that goes from the top left of the desk to the bottom right. A proper left-handed paper angle goes from the top right of the desk to the bottom left. The forearm of the child should be parallel to this angle to pass as right or left. See Photo 10.

Papers placed straight up and down on the desk or forearms which are not parallel with the paper are recorded as *fail* on this test. Improper angle, or a straight up and down paper, are also recorded as *fail*.

	Pass	Fail
	———	———

7. Reading

Now have your child read aloud for you. Give him something to read in which he can read about half the words and has difficulty with the remaining half. Try various reading materials until you find a book which presents approximately this amount of difficulty. When you are satisfied that he reads about half the words well and half poorly, take a 3″ x 5″ card, and place it about two inches in front of his *right* eye, so that he cannot see the book with the *right* eye.

Have him read for three minutes. Then place the cardboard about two inches in front of his *left* eye, so that he cannot see the book with his *left* eye. Have him read for three minutes. Keep a count of the number of words he can read with each eye. Do this test three times, keeping a record of the number of words which he can read with each eye on each test during the three-minute period. Now add the scores of the three right eye tests and the three left eye tests. The eye which read more words is the better eye in reading. If it is the *right* eye, record it as *right*; if the *left* eye read the most words, record *left*; if they are equal, record it as mixed.

Right	Left	Mixed
———	———	———

You can now record and summarize his eyedness as follows:

	Right	Left	Mixed
1. Looking through tube at distance	_____	_____	_____
2. Sighting through a hole in a sheet of paper	_____	_____	_____
3. Looking through a peep-hole at his desk	_____	_____	_____
4. Looking through a tube at his desk	_____	_____	_____
5. Writing position	_____	_____	_____
6. Paper angle	_____	_____	_____
7. Reading	_____	_____	_____

In order to have the proper eyedness for reading, your child's eyedness should be all right or all left on these tests. The all right should correspond to all right for handedness; the all left should correspond to all left for handedness.

D—*Earedness*

1. *Near Hearing*

Hold a watch under the center of the desk at which your child is seated. Ask him to put an ear on the desk top to see if he can hear the watch through the desk top. Record which ear he places on the desk top to listen. Move to the other side of the desk and repeat the test, asking your child to see if he can hear the watch through the desk top. Repeat this test three times and record which ear he places on the desk top. To be *right,* he must place the *right* ear on the desk top three times out of three; to be *left* he must place the *left* ear on the desk top three times out of three; otherwise, record him as *mixed.*

2. *Far Hearing*

Ask your child to get up from the desk and go to an inside wall of the room. Ask him to see if he can hear what is going on in the next room by placing an ear against the wall and listening. Record which ear he places against the wall. Have him come back to the desk; then repeat the test. Do this test three times, recording which ear he places against the wall for listening.

To be recorded as *right,* he must use his *right* ear for listening three times out of three; to be recorded as *left,* he must use his *left* ear three times out of three; otherwise, record him as mixed.

	Right	Left	Mixed
Near Hearing (watch test)	_____	_____	_____
Far Hearing (wall test)	_____	_____	_____

E—*Tonality*

The final test is an evaluation of your child's musical ability and appreciation. Musical ability is controlled in the sub-dominant hemisphere of the brain. A number of children with reading problems have greater musical ability and appreciation than do good readers.

Music activities, which stimulate the sub-dominant hemisphere of the brain, tend to interfere with the establishment of a dominant hemisphere. Children who excel at music, and children who are greatly *attracted* to music, sometimes have difficulty in establishing complete dominance. For the best result, when we begin to train for dominance, we have to decrease the amount of music in the child's environment during the training period. The easiest way to ascertain his musical ability, if he attends school, is to ask his music teacher. We have found that music teachers learn very quickly whether a child is very good or very poor at music. If you cannot see the music teacher, compare the amount of time your child spends listening to records or music with the amount spent by the children of your friends, who are of the same age. Does he listen to more music than do other children his age? Record your answer:

	Yes	No
Too musical	_____	_____

You can now summarize your child's development:

	Pass	Fail
Stage 1		
A. Sleep pattern	————	————
B. Visual pursuit	————	————
Stage 2		
A. Cross-pattern creeping	————	————
B. Vision	————	————
C. Visual pursuit	————	————
Stage 3		
A. Cross-pattern walking	————	————
B. Running	————	————
C. Visual pursuit	————	————
D. Head-paper distance	————	————
Stage 4		

These tests are recorded right, left or mixed.

	Right	Left	Mixed
A. *Handedness*			
1. Writing or crayoning	————	————	————
2. Eating	————	————	————
3. Throwing	————	————	————
4. Picking up objects	————	————	————
5. Brushing his teeth	————	————	————
6. Doing jigsaw puzzles	————	————	————
7. Pounding with a hammer	————	————	————
8. Cutting with scissors	————	————	————
9. Throwing darts	————	————	————
B. *Footedness*			
1. Kicking a ball	————	————	————
2. Picking up marbles	————	————	————
3. Foot-writing	————	————	————

C. *Eyedness*

1. Looking through tube at distance   _____   _____   _____

2. Sighting through a hole in a sheet of paper   _____   _____   _____

3. Looking through a tube at his desk   _____   _____   _____

4. Looking through a peep-hole at his desk   _____   _____   _____

5. Writing position   _____   _____   _____

6. Paper angle   _____   _____   _____

7. Reading   _____   _____   _____

D. *Earedness*

1. Near hearing   _____   _____   _____

2. Far hearing   _____   _____   _____

E. *Tonality*

You have now completed an evaluation of your child's development. If there are no *yes* answers in Stage 1, 2, and 3 your child has passed all of these tests and, if he is *all right or all left* in Stage 4, your child has passed this test and, therefore, his development is not interfering with his reading progress. If you have *yes* answers in Stages 1, 2, and 3, or if your child's sidedness is not all right or all left, he needs an opportunity to go back over the stages he has not completed.

Look back over his test results in Stages 1, 2, and 3. If he has failed a single test at any stage, he needs practice at that stage. Therapy starts at the lowest stage at which he failed a single test. If he is not completely right- or left-sided in Stage 4, he will need practice to become one-sided.

Failure of these tests indicates that your child needs further development if he is to become a good reader. We must take him back in his development to the earliest stage and give him the opportunity for that development.

Now is the time to stop practicing with his reading and to

start developing those areas of his nervous system that are blocking his progress in reading. It is futile to keep tutoring to try to help him with his reading until his nervous system is more ready to learn to read.

Chapter 12

TREATING THE PROBLEM:
THERAPY—STEPS 1, 2, AND 3

You ARE now ready to work at the *cause* of your child's reading problem. You must remember that your child is just as upset as you are, if not more so, about his poor reading. Before beginning the training program discuss the problem with him. Don't preach at him. Discuss his reading problem realistically, and ask him if he would like to improve his reading.

Explain to your child in general terms that you are going to use a developmental approach to his reading problem. Depending on his age and understanding, explain to him the basic ideas of this book. Tell him that together you are going back to the lowest stage of development at which he failed a single test, and that you will move forward stage by stage to the final stage of complete one-sidedness. Go over with him the stages at which he has failed a single test and explain what you will be doing at each stage.

We found that the best results are achieved when children follow our program under the supervision of their parents. Depending on your child's reaction and your schedule, arrange to have both his mother and father carry out the program. If this is impossible, one parent can carry out the program but it will be very helpful if the other parent is interested and enthusiastic. To be most effective, the program must be carried out seven days a week. Stopping the program for weekends delays progress and should be avoided, if at all possible.

Generally, cooperation is excellent when the explanation has been adequate. *If your child resists the ideas (1) that he has a reading problem and (2) that he should do something to correct it, he probably will not cooperate. Without his cooperation, the program will be extremely difficult to carry out and will be ineffective. When he expresses a willingness to work with you at home on a program aimed at increasing his ability to perform at school, you can begin.*

Since this program is very different from anything he has undertaken before, start it out as fun. You will be asked on many occasions, "What does this have to do with reading?" Be sure that you answer all his questions as factually as possible. Above all, be sure that you are not letting this program interfere with his pleasures, such as watching TV or playing outdoors.

You must fit in the program at a time which he will not resent losing. Carry out the program with only parents and your child in the room. Arrange a place where he will not be seen by other members of the family. More important, select a place where he will not be observed by his friends if they should drop in to visit. Pick a time and place that do not interfere with school, friends, or play.

Later, as he shows progress, he might *want* others to see what he is doing and learning, but this should be *his* decision, not yours.

Before you start, plan the entire program, one stage at a time. Spend no less than three weeks and *no more than six* on each of the first three stages. Be alert for signs of progress; the first signs are likely to occur in the athletic and coordination areas. Be sure to indicate the progress to your child. Such success will make it easier for him to maintain his enthusiasm. Another indication of progress will be in the appearance of his handwriting. Be sure that *he* notices the difference. The next area of improvement will be in his reading. Spelling improvement comes only after the reading has improved. The entire family should be told of progress in each area as it occurs.

Follow all the activities of one stage until that stage is completely mastered. After the mastery of each stage, write a report to be placed in your file. This report should list areas of progress. After a stage is mastered, take a few days' vacation, then move on to the next and follow all the activities of that stage. *Do not combine the activities of more than one stage at one time.*

Before you start the program, stop all tutoring or extra reading practice that you are giving your child. Do not attempt to change anything which the school is doing but, *when he starts this program, eliminate as much pressure about reading as possible.*

Remember that if your child fails a single test at any stage he must complete all the activities for that stage. Start at the lowest stage at which he missed a single test.

Stage 1

If your child failed a test at this level, start training him here. The therapy of Stage 1 consists of:

1. One-sided crawling	5 minutes
2. Sleep position	
3. Hearing practice	8 minutes
4. Visual practice	8 minutes
Total	21 minutes per day.

Remember, spend not less than three weeks nor more than six weeks at this stage.

1. *One-Sided Crawling*

Have him practice crawling. This is done by having him lie down on his stomach on a smooth surface, changing his position back and forth and sliding forward. Counting will help him to establish good rhythm. He should change smoothly from the right-sided position to the left, and continue. Show him Photos 1 and 2 which show the starting positions for crawling, which are the same as the sleeping positions.

Once he has the idea that the left arm and leg are forward when his right arm and leg are down, teach him to reverse the process. When this is done, teach him to alternate these motions as smoothly and as quietly as possible as he crawls.

As he learns to crawl, teach him to turn his head and look at the hand which comes up at each turn. When his left hand is up he turns his head and looks at it, when the right hand is up, he turns his head and looks at it.

Watch him as he does the crawling. Be sure that he keeps the proper rhythm. A smooth surface, such as linoleum, makes it easy to slide along the floor. Be sure that his head turns smoothly. As he begins to look at each hand, he is beginning to use his eyes at this stage. Practice this for five minutes per day.

2. *Sleep Position*

Once each night place him in the proper sleep position. First, teach him to sleep on his stomach. To do this, wait until he is asleep, then gently roll him over onto his stomach once each night, preferably when you go to bed. If he uses a pillow, have him use one of medium size, because large pillows tend to discourage sleeping on one's stomach. When you have him sleeping on his stomach regularly, begin to place him in a proper sleep pattern each night, after he is asleep or when you go to bed. Do this once each night. See the proper position for left- and right-handers in Photos 1 and 2.

3. *Hearing*

To train his hearing at this stage, have him cover his right ear with his right hand so that he cannot hear with his right ear. Now talk to him and have him respond, with his right ear not hearing. Next, have him cover his left ear with his left hand while you carry on a conversation with him.

These one-eared conversations with him listening to you and

talking to you, help him to reinforce his alternate one-sidedness in hearing at this stage.

Have him practice this with each ear for four one-minute periods per day.

4. *Visual Practice*

Your child now can begin some visual exercises typical of this stage. If he normally wears glasses, have him wear them for this practice.

Have your child cover his left eye with his left hand. Put a small flashlight, or some interesting object, in his right hand at arm's length and have him move it around in all directions, circularly, up and down, and from side to side. At the same time, have him look at the object with his right eye. He is following his right hand with his right eye, and, with practice, should learn to do so smoothly. Have him do this for four one-minute periods per day.

Next have him cover his right eye with his right hand. Moving the flashlight, or other object, with his left hand, he now follows his left hand with his left eye. Have him do this for four one-minute periods per day. He should be able to follow his own hand smoothly, with practice.

Spend at least three weeks at this stage. If, at the end of that time, your child performs all these activities perfectly, you are ready to move up to the next stage. If not, continue until he improves; however, do not spend more than six weeks at this stage.

When your child has completed this stage, write a short report of his performance for your files and give your child a vacation for a few days. Then move on to Stage 2.

Stage 2

This stage represents good use of both sides of the body. If your child failed a test at this stage, start him on the following activities:

1.	Cross-pattern creeping	30 minutes
2.	Hearing practice (speech)	4 minutes
3.	Hearing practice (reading)	15 minutes
4.	Visual practice	4 minutes
	Total	53 minutes

Spend not less than three weeks nor more than six at this stage.

1. *Cross-Pattern Creeping*

This is much more complex than it seems. Buy or make your child a pair of knee pads, or have him practice on a thick rug. Have him remove his shoes for creeping practice. Get down on the floor with him and teach him how to creep slowly and properly. The first goal is to have him creep so that the opposite hand and knee touch the floor at the same time. That is, as the *right* hand touches the floor so should the *left* knee; and as the *left* hand touches the floor so should the *right* knee. Work on smoothing out the creeping until this opposite—or cross—pattern is achieved. When it is, begin to refine the creeping as follows. Be sure that he does each part perfectly.

a. Teach the child to *look at his forward hand as he creeps*. First the right hand, then the left. Have him turn his head slightly toward the forward hand as he looks at it.

b. Be sure that the palms of his hands are flat and that the fingers point straight forward.

c. *Never allow the knees to cross*. Be sure that the knees are at least eight to twelve inches apart as he creeps.

d. Be sure he raises his knees with each forward step and be sure that he drags his feet. His knees are raised with each step, but his feet, shoeless, are in constant contact with the floor. This should be done for three separate ten-minute periods per day. Schedule these periods so that there is at least one hour between each.

2. *Hearing Practice*

A. Hearing practice at this stage consists of the child listening with both ears while the speaker changes position. Have your child sit in a chair in the middle of the room, then carry on a conversation with him, but move slowly around the room as you talk. Your child will be able to see you for part of the conversation but will not be able to see you when you are behind him. Be sure he does not turn his head to follow you as you move. He is learning to place sound in space, while at times seeing the source of the sound and at times not. Carry on this hearing practice for four minutes per day.

B. Spend some time daily reading aloud to your child at this stage. If possible, read to him for fifteen minutes per day. Read stories that are of interest to him, even though they may be too difficult for him to read independently. If you must, of necessity, *read* the homework for your child. An additional five or ten minutes of reading stories is helpful at this stage. Alternate your position for reading, at times sitting to the right of your child, at times to his left, and at other times directly in front of him.

3. *Visual Practice*

Have your child hold a small flashlight, or an interesting object, in his writing hand. Have him hold it at arm's length and move it in all directions, following it with both his eyes. Periodically have him bring the light up to his nose, trying to see how close to his nose his eyes can follow it. As he gains smoothness in following the light, have him bring the light closer to his face to do the exercise. Gradually have him move it closer so that he can follow the light smoothly with both eyes when the light is about twelve inches from his face. This should be done for four one-minute periods per day.

Spend at least three weeks at this stage. If, at the end of three weeks, he performs all these activities perfectly you are ready to move on to the next stage. If not, have him continue practice at this stage, but do not go beyond a total of six weeks.

When your child has mastered this stage, write a short report for your files, describing his present performance. You will now begin to see areas of improvement, especially in coordination, which you will want to record. After a few days' vacation, move on to the next stage.

Stage 3

If he failed a test at this stage, he will have the following program:

1.	Cross-pattern walking	20 minutes
2.	Hearing practice	8 minutes
3.	General coordination practice	30 minutes
4.	Visual practice	8 minutes
5.	Right-left orientation	10 minutes
	Total	76 minutes

Spend not less than three weeks nor more than six at this stage.

1. *Cross-Pattern Walking*

In teaching cross-pattern walking you must start slowly. Have your child take a step with his *left* foot and have him point to it with his right hand. This will be easier if he turns slightly at the waist. Next, have him take a step with his right foot and point at it with his left hand. As he walks, he points to the left foot with his right hand, and to his right foot with his left hand, with the upper body turned slightly toward the foot at which he is pointing. Show him Photos 6 and 7.

When he has mastered the cross-pattern walking and can point easily to the opposite foot with alternate hands, teach him to *look at the forward hand consistently.*

As he becomes a fairly good cross-pattern walker, add the following:

a. Have him practice in bare or stocking feet.
b. Have him toe out slightly.
c. Be sure his feet are at least ten inches apart.
d. Vary the speed from slower than usual to fast, then back to slow.

Your child should practice this for twenty minutes per day in ten-minute periods, for a minimum of three weeks.

If you have difficulty teaching him to cross-pattern walk, go back to cross-pattern creeping practice for a week or two, and then teach him the walking again.

2. *Hearing Practice*

Hearing practice at this stage can take the form of games. First, have your child sit in a chair in the middle of the room, *with both eyes closed*. Walk around the room talking to him. Periodically, as you move, ask him to point to where he thinks you are. Since he is not seeing, he must localize your voice in the room by ear. He is learning to place sound at various distances and localities in space.

Another hearing game to play at this stage is a word recognition game. Seat your child in a chair *with his eyes open,* and have him look straight ahead. Stand behind him and ask him to tell you whether the words, which you are going to *whisper* to him, are alike or different. Start the game with words which are obviously different from each other, such as "dog" and "bike." Alternate these with words which are the same, "dog" and "dog." Gradually change the unlike words so that the differences are not so obvious, for example, "wet-went," "hair-share," "smile-mile," "ten-pen." After each pair, ask him whether they were alike or different. To keep the game interesting, periodically insert two that *are alike*. This game helps to create more refined hearing at this stage. Practice each of these games four minutes each day.

3. *Visual Training*

If your child normally wears glasses, have him wear them for this training. Take a small flashlight, or other interesting small object, in *your* hand, and have your child look at it with both eyes while you move it about in space. Move the object in all directions, up and down, side to side, up and down at an angle, and in a circle. Be sure that he moves only his eyes and not his head, to follow your hand. Occasionally vary the distance from your hand to his eyes. Occasionally during each session move your hand slowly up to within four inches from his eyes. Ask him to follow the object as closely as possible. Do this for four one-minute sessions per day.

As he improves at following with both eyes the object in your hand, you may begin to decrease the time spent on that activity. Instead, teach him to look at objects on command. Start at the dinner table with "Look at Dad," "look at your plate," "look at the ceiling," "look at the window." As this improves, play this game in other environments. It is also beneficial outdoors.

4. *General Coordination*

By this stage you will be able to see improvement in your child's general coordination. Try to spend as much time playing outdoor games with him as possible. Praise him for the improvements you see. Games involving running and jumping are valuable. Be sure that all his running is in cross-pattern. Show him how to use his arms and hands in a "pumping" motion to gain speed in running. This also helps his running to be in a cross-pattern.

Have him watch people walking and running. Point out to him the cross-pattern which people use when they walk. Explain that this is what he has been practicing and that this is the way in which he should walk at all times.

If your child cannot jump or ride a bicycle, he should be taught to do so now. Running, jumping, and bike-riding are excellent for his coordination; they are also helpful in the development of speed in vision. Try to spend thirty minues daily on outdoor activities with your child during this stage.

5. *Right-Left Orientation*

You are now ready to teach your child the *idea* of right and left so that each is automatic to him.

While he walks or runs in cross-pattern, say, "turn right" or "turn left," as a game in which you are trying to fool him. He may have a little difficulty at first, but with encouragement and practice he should be able to master right-left orientation. Practice this for ten minutes per day.

When your child has spent at least three weeks at this stage and does all these activities perfectly, stop and write a short report of his progress for your file. If he is not perfect, have him continue until he is, but do not continue beyond a total of six weeks.

You have now taken your child through the first three stages of development. He is now ready to move on to the final stage, in which he will achieve complete one-sidedness.

Chapter 13

TREATING THE PROBLEM:
THERAPY—STEP 4

You NOW must help your child to become completely one-sided. That is, he should be consistently right-handed, right-footed, right-eared and right-eyed, *or* he should be left-handed, left-footed, left-eared and left-eyed. If in your evaluation of your child's development he was all right-sided or all left-sided, he does not need practice at this stage. If he was not, *he will need practice only in those activities in which he was not completely one-sided*. Go back over your summary on pages 123–124 to see in which area (hand, foot, ear, or eye) he was not completely one-sided. Do only those parts of the program which are applicable. Remember, if he is right-handed, everything should test right—foot, ear, and eye; or, if he is left-handed, everything should test left—foot, ear, and eye.

Discuss sidedness with your child, explaining that complete one-sidedness is the objective. His cooperation is essential if he is to learn to use his one side exclusively for all activities, including sports.

Start this stage by eliminating music from your child's environment as much as is practicable; he should not be allowed to listen to the radio or phonograph at home.

Television presents a knotty problem. We have learned to compromise on the use of television, allowing the child to watch as much as one hour per day. The programs, however, should not be strictly musical programs. Since all television programs have musical backgrounds, try to have the picture as clear and bright as possible but turn down the sound volume so that it can *just* be heard and understood.

Children whose development is not complete at this stage tend to turn up the television volume so that it is much too loud. The objective at this stage is to *decrease* the amount of music which your child hears. This includes his own singing, humming, or whistling, which should be discouraged. It is wise *not* to tamper with his school music activities, so do not attempt to make any changes in his school curriculum.

Treatment at this stage is as follows:

1. Handedness activities, for which there are no time requirements. These activities can be followed as part of your child's daily living.
2. Writing (if required)   10 to 40 minutes
3. Throwing (if required)   10 minutes
4. Footedness   15 minutes
5. Earedness   10 minutes
6. Winking   4 minutes
7. Sighting   4 minutes
8. Target sighting   4 minutes
9. Peephole practice   4 minutes

Because Stage 4 is the highest level of development it usually requires more time for mastery. Spend not less than six weeks nor more than ten weeks at Stage 4.

1. *Handedness*

Generally, unless your child has been forced by you or by his school into using a specific hand for writing, it is wise to accept his *writing hand* as his handedness. Most children who spontaneously choose a hand for writing are indicating their true handedness.

In the past, some parents and schools have arbitrarily assigned a handedness to a child. If this handedness was not the child's natural handedness, reading problems occurred and, in some instances, stuttering resulted. As a general rule, the writing hand is a good indication of handedness unless there has been interference. If your child writes with one hand, without having been forced to do so, but does many other activities with the other hand, it is usually wise to accept his writing hand as the indication of his true sidedness.

If, however, your child writes equally well with either hand, use all the other indications of sidedness to decide on his handedness. For example, if he writes equally well with both hands and, if he is right-eyed, right-footed and right-eared, he will most likely react best to being exclusively right-handed for writing.

In the past, a number of truly left-handed children were *made* into reading problems through being forced to be right-handed. These children rarely become completely right-handed and, as a result, they are quite mixed when evaluated for handedness. Quite often they write quite well with their natural left hand, even though most of their writing has been done with the right hand.

The decision to make at this stage is *which is his natural sidedness?* In a few instances this is a difficult decision. *If your child is extremely mixed in all handedness activities, including writing, consult your doctor and your school for help in making the decision.* For the great majority of children, however, the natural sidedness of a child is relatively easily gauged. The most common problem is that he does most things which his natural hand, but does not do *everything* with that hand. Look over the tests of handedness to see what your child's natural handedness is. Remember that the writing hand is an excellent indication, unless it has been forced. When you have ascertained his hand choice, your work begins. You must train him to use that hand exclusively for all skills. Remember, if your child is one of those children whose *writing hand should be changed, consult with your family doctor and school before making such a change.*

Start by teaching him to do exclusively the following with the hand which you want to be dominant. Remember, he is to be *all right* or *all left*.

a. Eating—Have him use his tableware—knife, fork, spoon, and glass—with the proper hand. When setting the table, place all these utensils on the same side of his plate to eliminate the opportunity to use them with both hands.

b. Drinking—Always place his glass on the proper side of the plate and always insist that he hold his glass with his proper hand.

c. Brushing teeth—Be sure that he always holds his toothbrush in his proper hand.

d. Picking up things—Watch him as he uses his hands in picking up things. Remind him to use his proper hand.

e. Touch discrimination—If he seems to have trouble in developing a "dominant hand," you might try this. Have him close his eyes, then place a small object in his hand (paper clip, rubber band, match box, or marble) and ask him to identify it. He will have to recognize it through feeling. This helps to set up hand-brain pathways of a sensory or feeling nature.

2. *Writing*

If your child writes poorly with his dominant hand, he will profit from some extra writing practice. You can decide whether or not to do this writing practice on the basis of your child's teachers' report about his writing. Buy a four-feet-square piece of plywood and paint it with green blackboard paint, which can be purchased at most hardware stores. The painted plywood now becomes a very large chalkboard. Also buy a box of chalk in assorted colors. Have your child stand facing the wall. Have him stand up straight and touch his chin to the wall. Mark the spot where his chin touches the wall. Use this spot to mark the exact *center* of the chalkboard when it is fastened to the wall. Now fasten it securely.

Your child should always stand when writing on the chalkboard. Be sure that he stands straight and does not lean on anything.

Now have him write the words which he can read, on the chalkboard, copying them. Do not dictate them and expect him to be able to write them. Allow him to write in any size he chooses, over one inch in size. If he is not able to write on a reasonably straight line, place one permanent horizontal line on the blackboard for him. This is most easily done with a strip of half-inch adhesive tape. The tape is durable and can be changed easily. The adhesive strip, which becomes the line on which your child's writing rests, should be placed as follows: Have your child stand facing the chalkboard and have him touch his chin to it. This point is the exact height for the strip (which will, of course, be at the center of the board). Place it horizontally across the blackboard at this height. Explain to your child that the adhesive strip will be the baseline of the words which he will write. Keep the practice sessions of writing at ten minutes or less. You may have as many as four sessions per day, depending on how poorly your child writes.

3. *Throwing*

The most difficult handedness task to teach is throwing. The secret is to start slowly with underhand throwing. This can be done indoors. Let us assume that your child is right-handed in all activities but throws with his left hand, and now is to be taught to throw right-handed.

Start with having him gently throw a small rubber ball to you, *underhanded*, with his right hand. Next teach him to place his *right foot forward*, as though he were a pitcher, whenever he throws the ball. When he has learned to start with his right foot forward, place your hand on top of his right foot and have him throw. As he throws, his right foot will be unable to move because of your hand. This will encourage movement of the left foot—the proper foot for a right-handed throw. Encourage him to raise and step forward with his left foot as he throws. As he becomes better he will step forward with the left foot naturally, ending in a cross-pattern.

For left-handers the left foot is placed forward and made immobile. As the left hand moves backward to throw the ball, the right foot moves forward, again ending in a cross-pattern. This is made easier by added practice at cross-pattern walking. See Photos 14, 15, and 16.

Practice throwing ten minutes per day, if needed.

The development of complete one-sidedness for hand use is at times a slow and difficult process. You may find yourself nagging your child about it. *Encourage the use of the proper hand, rather than discourage the use of the other hand,* Try to keep nagging at a minimum. Remember that your child is establishing new channels in the brain and this takes time.

4. *Footedness*

Now he also can begin to establish footedness. You must train the foot to be dominant on the same side as handedness. This can be started with such activities as picking up marbles with the toes of the foot which you want to make the dominant foot. This can be expanded into picking up with the toes more difficult objects. This can be fun but it also can be exasperating, so move slowly. Next teach your child to hold a pencil or, if it is easier, a large crayon, between his big toe and the next toe. Have him try to draw with the proper foot. He will find this extremely difficult at first. You might try it yourself, if he needs some extra encouragement.

Now you can proceed to kicking as part of footedness training. Start with a soccer-type ball which you place on the ground. Have your child run up to it slowly and kick it with the proper foot. Next have him increase running speed as he approaches the ball.

Gradually diminish the size of the ball which he kicks until he can kick a small rubber ball consistently with the proper foot.

Now you can use games, such as soccer and football, to con-

tinue this practice. The objective is to have your child consistently use the foot on the same side as his handedness for all
these activities. Spend fifteen minutes per day on these activities.

5. *Earedness*

If the tests indicate that his earedness is different from his
handedness, he needs training in this area. Spend two five-minute periods each day talking to or reading to your child. While
you are sitting on his right side, ask him to cover his left ear
while he listens to you. If he is left-handed, sit on his left side
and ask him to cover his right ear as he listens. Do this for two
five-minute periods per day.

As your child begins to master one-sided hand, ear, and foot
use, you can add the following visual training to his program.

6. *Winking*

Teach your child to wink the eye opposite from his handedness. Some children find it difficult to wink. Teach your child
to wink on command. At first he might close both eyes as he
attempts to wink. With practice he will learn to wink his sub-
dominant eye, while keeping his dominant eye open.

Practice this for four one-minute periods per day.

7. *Sighting*

Teach your child to use a telescope or microscope. If these
are not available, use a paper tube. Have him look through it
with his dominant eye. Teach him to close the other eye while
looking through the telescope or microscope.

Have him practice bringing the telescope directly to the proper
eye without making a shift from one eye to the other. Have him
practice walking up to a microscope and placing the proper eye
on the eye-piece until he is able to do so without hesitation.

He should learn to bring a telescope up to the correct eye
without any hesitation, or he should be able to walk up to a
microscope and place the proper eye on it without hesitation.

When he has mastered this, have him practice sighting *while both eyes are open*. That is, have him bring the telescope up to his proper eye without closing the sub-dominant eye.

He should practice sighting four one-minute periods per day.

8. *Target Sighting*

Set up a small target at one end of a room. To make the target, put a large X on a sheet of paper. Have your child stand at the other end of the room. With the forefinger of his dominant hand, have him aim at the target while he closes his sub-dominant eye, as though he were shooting at it with his finger. Practice sighting the target with your child. Explain how aiming occurs, and teach him to close his sub-dominant eye while aiming.

When he has learned how to aim, buy him a toy pistol which shoots a cork, rubber pellets, or rubber-tipped darts. Have him practice shooting at the target. Remind him to aim with his dominant eye and to keep the sub-dominant eye closed while aiming. After a little practice, his shooting score will improve dramatically. Next, teach him to do his shooting while keeping *both* eyes open.

Have him practice sighting and shooting for four one-minute periods per day.

9. *Peephole Practice*

Use a pencil point to push a small hole, no more than ¼ inch in diameter, into the middle of a sheet of cardboard. Have your child practice looking through this hole with his *dominant* eye, while holding the cardboard at arm's length. Have him sight different objects through the hole. As he becomes proficient, increase the speed with which you name the objects he is to sight. Choose objects which are at varying distances from him. Practice this for four one-minute periods per day.

You have now given your child's nervous system a new opportunity to develop. He is now ready to profit from help in reading, but first we must set the stage.

Chapter 14

SETTING THE STAGE

CHILDREN WHO have reading problems quite often never learn what reading is *for*. Reading, to them, is a frightening, failure-producing school subject which has no relationship to life. Even though your child has now reached the stage where he can learn to read, because of his history of failure no doubt he now has quite a negative attitude toward reading. Such children read when they have to, but rarely read for pleasure, because there is no real pleasure in their struggle to read. Not only is there no pleasure, but also there is not much use to which they can put their reading. Such children avoid reading, and read only when commanded or forced.

At this point we must set the stage to help your child see that reading *can* be useful to him and that on some occasions reading can even be fun. In the old days we could entice him to read comic strips in newspapers or comic books. This isn't very seductive today, especially when compared to the readily available cartoons on television. Previously, we might have enticed him to read the sports page of the newspaper, but alas, he can now watch the entire sporting event on television and doesn't need to read about it.

Children not only need to learn to read, but they need to learn what reading is for. Reading only when forced to do so results in very little reading. Practice is necessary in reading as in most learned skills. The more a child reads, the easier it is to read. Helping children to want to learn to read independently is helped, we have found, by some enticing. We have found the following ideas helpful in encouraging children to read more, oftener, and to learn that reading can be a helpful activity. Read over these suggestions. Select a few which you think might be enticing to your child and set the stage.

1. *The Television Section from the Local Newspaper*

The daily and weekly television program listings seem to present few obstacles to reading. Place the weekly T.V. schedule which is included in the Sunday edition, in a place which is easily available. A felt-tipped pen is helpful so that each child can read the schedule, then circle those programs which he is interested in seeing. Perhaps each child in the family could use a different colored felt-tipped pen to identify his preferences, thus eliminating any conflicts of scheduling in advance. A little discussion of family T.V. rules beforehand may help.

2. *Articles of Interest*

Cut out magazine articles which you feel might be of interest to your child. Staple the entire article together and deliver it to his bedside table. You might have your older children go through the magazines searching for articles which might interest their younger siblings, or your problem reader. Such articles should not be considered "required reading"; they should just be available on the bedside table.

3. *Mailing Lists*

There are a number of magazines which carry advertisements such as the following:

"Do you want to receive more mail? Send us 50 cents and we will see that your name is put on many mailing lists." *

In the United States the mail order business is big business.

* See advertisements in *Popular Science, Popular Mechanics,* and *Science Illustrated.*

Companies prepare beautiful mailing pieces. They spend considerable amounts of money *buying* lists of names of people to whom they can send their mailing pieces.

It is almost impossible for even a non-reading child to ignore an attractive piece of mail which is addressed to him, personally.

I know one family in which the children's names have been placed on so many mailing lists by their parents that the postman delivers the childrens' mail in small sacks. These children spend hours each week *reading* the mail which has been delivered to them.

4. *International Mail*

There are a number of international mail order houses. These mail out attractive and highly educational mailing pieces.

Once again, check through magazine advertisements to put your child's name on an international mailing list. Soon he will begin to receive exotic mail from various parts of the world. It will be difficult for him to resist reading foreign mail addressed to him personally.

These international mailings are highly informative about the countries from which they emanate. I suggest that you look at the mail yourself after your child has finished perusing it. You may find yourself fascinated.

5. *The Local Newspaper*

Reading about people and places you know is more exciting than reading about strange faces and places. If your community has a small, local newspaper be sure to enter a subscription. Discuss community events which are reported. Keep the paper in a spot which is readily accessible to all family members. Kitchens and bathrooms are good places for leaving materials to be read.

6. *Instructions*

Save all instruction sheets which come with things you buy. Keep the sheets in a drawer, consider the drawer an Instruction

Sheets Drawer. Among the instruction sheets kept there should be instructions which you received with appliances, T.V., lawn mowers, automobiles, radios, phonographs, razors, and also laundering instructions for many items of clothing. Almost everything you buy these days is accompanied by a set of written instructions. Save the tags and keep them in one specific drawer in the house. Whenever your child uses an appliance or questions its use, refer him to the "Instructions Drawer."

7. *Large Mail Order Catalogues*

Historically, rural children have spent hours paging through Sears, Roebuck or Montgomery Ward catalogues. Today there are many more such catalogues. Arrange to receive all of them by mail, have them addressed to your child, and keep them all handy. Casual paging through the catalogues to look at the pictures often leads to reading, when a child sees a picture of something he would like. Be sure to obtain the L. L. Bean, Orvis, and Eddie Bauer's * catalogues for the sportsmen of the family. You might also benefit from consulting Elizabeth Squire's *The Mail Order Shopping Guide*, published by M. Barrows and Company, New York, N.Y. Needless to say, any home with children should always have the current catalogue from F.A.O. Schwarz, the toy store at 745 Fifth Avenue, New York, N.Y., 10022.

8. *Trips and Excursions*

Planning for trips, vacations, or excursions to nearby points of interest should be preceded by systematic accumulation of maps, folders, and descriptions of the area to be visited.

Gasoline stations have free maps for your use. Gasoline companies and automobile associations prepare mile by mile descriptive sheets about your route to your destination. These routing services are provided free of charge. Send for them.

Write to the local Chamber of Commerce to request descrip-

---

* Of Freeport, Maine, Manchester, Vt., and Seattle, Wash.

tive material about your destination, and to the Chambers of the towns en route.

Have your children look over all the materials to make suggestions about the forthcoming trip. Each member of the family who has participated in the arrangements for the trip will become a more enthusiastic traveler, particularly if he has become interested enough in some of the locations to do some reading about them before the departure.

9. *Personal Subscriptions*

A child who has a reading problem should have at least one subscription to a magazine. There are numerous childrens' magazines available by subscription. Teen-age magazines are also readily available. Generally it is difficult to ignore a magazine which is addressed to you personally and which arrives regularly.

10. *Magic-Marker Treatment*

Whenever you read a magazine or newspaper have a light-colored felt-tipped pen nearby. As you read sections, paragraphs, or even sentences which you feel might interest your non-reading child, circle the material with your felt-tipped pen. Say nothing to the child but leave the newspaper or magazine around the house where it will be available.

11. *Grocery Orders*

There is always much discussion, both pro and con, about food in the family. Requests for food should be made in writing. Keep a food list on your bulletin board or near the kitchen telephone. Require that any requests for special foods be written on the list. You will notice that new foods are placed on the list and that the list will be read to see what foods have been listed by others in the family.

12. *Bulletin Board*

Hang a bulletin board on a convenient wall at a height accessible to all family members. Try to place as many written messages as possible on the board. Invitations, interesting community activities, even cartoons can be used.

13. *Instruction Books*

The book most frequently read by teen-agers with reading problems is the Drivers' Manual. Obtaining a drivers license is important enough to most teen-agers so that they read and re-read the Drivers' Manual, hoping to pass the drivers test.

Do you have other instruction books which are important? What are your child's interests? Locate books on those subjects and make these books easily available to your child.

14. *Clean Out Your Attic*

Old school or college yearbooks, newspaper articles, or announcements about your life are often intriguing to your children. Old snapshots, old school books, or report cards can all make interesting reading for the younger generation. There will be laughter about the styles of your clothes and perhaps about hair fashions, but also there may be some reading.

15. *Sales Drawer*

Save all newspaper inserts and some full-page advertisements of sales. Discount houses and department stores periodically mail out catalogues. Place these in a drawer, the Sales Drawer. Whenever your child wants to buy something, have him go to the Sales Drawer to look up his item and to find the best place to buy it. If a child is directly involved, if he is to use his own money, and if he is buying something he wants very much, he is prone to read rather carefully before he buys.

16. *Your Home Town and State*

Write to your local Chamber of Commerce and to the State Chamber of Commerce regularly. Request descriptive material of the area where you live. It is interesting to learn local geography and history when it is camouflaged as tourist information.

Children find it difficult to resist reading about the history, geography, and tourist attractions of their own communities and state.

Remember that these suggestions have been aimed at setting the stage for reading. Select a few of them and try them.

Never insist that your child read the materials which you are making available. You are providing an opportunity for him to see the purpose of reading and you are making it easier for him to start to read for fun.

Chapter 15

TREATMENT—AND NOW TO READING

Now THAT YOUR child has gone through Stages 1 through 4 his brain should be more ready to deal with written words. You have set the stage for reading for fun. The introduction of supervised study at home now is very important.

Call your child's teacher and arrange another conference. Review your child's file before going. Start the conference by asking all the questions you asked at your original conference. Explain that you would like to set up a daily homework and supervised study program at home. If your child attends a school which frowns on homework you will have to procure books and workbooks elsewhere. Be sure to ask again what your child's grade level score in reading is at this time.

When you return home compare the notes from your previous conference with your present notes. Discuss with your child the changes which his teacher has noted. Also discuss with him the fact that you are now going to set up a daily supervised study and reading period. This will be his homework period. Depending on your child's age, this daily homework or reading period should vary from one-half hour daily, with children in first and second grade, to an hour or more for children from third grade on. Use your own judgment as to the exact amount. Having set an amount of time per day, the next step is to agree with your child on the time of day at which his supervised study period will start. Be sure that the time you set doesn't interfere with other activities or with recreation. Too often children rebel at homework because of time conflicts with other activities. Try to set a time which presents the least conflict.

Now choose a place. Most parents immediately choose the child's own room. This is often a poor choice because it is isolated. Remember, your child will need help and attention. Choose a place where a parent will be easily available when needed during the agreed upon study time. This might be the dining room or kitchen or it might be a bedroom, depending on where the available parent will be at the agreed upon homework time.

A proper desk is essential. Having your child help to choose a desk is usually helpful. At local dime stores it is often possible to obtain sturdy, but inexpensive, flat top desks made of formica and wrought iron. A father or older brother who is handy with tools might easily build one. An older child might build his own. Be sure that the desk chair is high enough so that he can retain the proper head-paper position as he works at his desk.

You will recall that his head should be held at a constant distance from his paper or book. This distance is measured by placing his elbow on the paper or book and making a fist. The first knuckle of the fist should come to your child's eyes. This is the proper head-paper distance which you want to teach him to use as consistently as possible. See Photo 10. This will take a lot of reminding. Children with reading problems very often hold their faces too close to their books.

You may find it helpful to place a pillow on his desk chair. This makes it easier for him to maintain the proper distance from his eye to the paper. Watch your child as he does anything requiring use of his eyes on close work—for example, eating, doing puzzles, crayoning, or model-making. Remind him of the proper head-paper distance in each of these activities. Do not allow him to lie down when he reads or writes. Do not allow him to put his head down on the desk as he writes. As you make progress in developing the proper head-paper distance, tactfully ask his teacher to remind him of it when he reads or writes at school.

After you establish the proper head-paper distance, establish the proper *angle-of-seeing* in writing. The proper angle for holding papers, when writing, is shown in Photo 10. Show the picture which fits his handedness to your child. Explain that this is the ideal and that you will begin to move him toward it slowly. Have him write sitting at his desk. Look at the angle at which he holds his paper. Rotate it slightly toward the proper position. Have him write again. If he continues to be comfortable in this position, use it as the first step in training him to use the ideal position.

Place a strip of white adhesive tape along the side edge of the paper at this angle and fasten it to his desk. He now has a guide against which he can place his paper whenever he writes. As he becomes comfortable with this angle, change the angle of the tape again, moving it slightly toward the ideal position.

Change the angle of his paper for writing very slowly, for you are not only establishing new habits, you are also breaking old habits. When he learns to hold his paper at the proper angle for writing, you have aligned his seeing for its most efficient use by standardizing the distance and the angle at which he sees.

If you don't have books of the proper level of difficulty, go to your library or department store book section, to the "easy-to-read" section. If your child is reading at a certain grade level —remember you asked his teacher about this—ask the clerk for books at this grade level. Try to find books that are written about his particular interests. This is relatively easy to do, for you know your child's interests better than anyone else, and there are many good books for children published each year.

If you have difficulty determining the proper grade level, use this rule of thumb. Take your child along to the bookstore. Choose an easy book which interests him. Open the book to a page at random and ask him to read it. If he misses *more* than two out of every ten words, the book is too difficult for him,

Have him read from a few books until you find one in which he misses *no more* than two out of ten words read. This is the proper difficulty level of books which he should read at this stage.

Be sure that each session takes place at your child's desk. Start with helping with homework, if there is any. First help your child to go over the entire assignment to see how much there is to do. If the reading is too difficult help your child with it. Often if a parent reads a page and then the child reads a page the child's attitude toward homework improves appreciably. At each session complete the homework *first* before going on to reading. Remember that completing his homework is very important to your child because he has to face his teacher and classmates the next day. Because of your help the homework will take less time than it did previously. As the homework completion becomes more efficient you can begin to add reading practice during this period.

There are three basic aspects of reading. The first is speed of reading. Speed is acquired through much practice with relatively easy reading material. As a child becomes familiar with more words his speed increases. When your child comes to a word he doesn't know, tell it to him. Don't force him to puzzle it out because he will lose his train of thought in the reading.

As your child gains confidence in his reading you might want to do the following to increase his speed. Take a piece of cardboard or paper which is cut to fit the width of an ordinary book. Have your child begin reading at the top of a page. As he reads move the cardboard down from the top of the page, covering the line he has just read. As he reads each line slide the cardboard down over it to cover it. As your child reads, you can hurry him slightly by moving the cardboard down a bit faster. Be sure to tell him that you are trying to hurry him a bit as you work at his speed. Do not hurry him so much that you upset him.

The second important aspect of reading is vocabulary. This

includes the number of words which your child can recognize and the meanings of words which he reads. You can help with this both during the study period and during discussion. Try to make him aware of word meanings. Whenever a word comes up in conversation or reading, explain its meaning to your child. Do this in as interesting a manner as possible, telling him where the word came from, how its meaning has changed over the years, as points of interest. You can also play family games where one member of the family says a word and the others tell what it means.

The most important aspect of reading is comprehension, or understanding what one is reading. There are a number of ways in which comprehension can be improved. These involve getting the child's brain ready to take in the information. Knowing what you are going to read about helps one to understand what one reads. This can be done in several ways.

Before he reads a book, tell your child what it is about. Tell him in general terms the plot, the location, and a bit about each character in the book. Go through the book with your child, discussing first the table of contents. Then go through and discuss titles as they appear in the book.

Discuss the pictures and illustrations in the book. Be sure to point out the relationship of the titles to the pictures. Before he reads a book, go through it, picking out key words. Teach him their meanings and to recognize them when they appear. Tell him that you are going to ask him a few sample questions about the book *before* he reads it. Ask him to try to keep these sample questions in mind while he reads. Now ask him questions about the main characters, the location of the action, and about the time that the action took place. After he has read a page ask him to tell you in his own words what he has read.

Remember—*each homework period begins with the completion of the work assigned by his teacher; then go on to his reading. Continue the evening homework sessions for a period of three months.*

You are now ready for another teacher conference. Ask the same questions and be sure to ask about reading scores. Many children will have overcome their reading problems at this point. Ask your child's teacher if she feels that he has overcome them. Compare her answer with your own appraisal.

You may ask, "I know he reads better but how do I know whether he has overcome his problem?" There are four basic indications that you can follow.

First, does he read with improved speed, vocabulary and understanding? Second, are his reading scores at school improved and are they at grade level? Third, is his report card satisfactory and, fourth, does he choose his own books (which are typical of his age level) to read for fun, without being forced to?

Reading material which he chooses, and obviously reading it with pleasure, is the best indication that he has overcome his problem. If your child has achieved all of these, stop supervising his homework and the reading periods. He no longer needs your help and will gain greater independence on his own.

There will be some children who reach this stage of treatment without achieving all four of these goals. For these remaining children move on to the next level of treatment.

Chapter 16

IF THE PROBLEM CONTINUES

GO BACK TO pages 123–124 to check the difference between your child's handedness and his dominant eye. Now *retest his handedness and eyedness,* as you did originally on pages 115–121.

If his eyedness continues to differ from his handedness, more training is indicated. Before you start, seek an appointment with a local eye doctor. There are two types. One is a medical doctor whose training is more physiological and disease oriented, called an ophthalmologist. The other is an optometrist, whose training is primarily in the areas of optics and visual training. Choose the one who is not too busy to sit down to discuss your child's problem with you.

Tell him what you have done and what the results have been. Tell him about your child's handedness and eyedness and ask him for suggestions. Following his examination of your child's vision, he will make suggestions to you about your child's vision. *Follow these suggestions.*

If he has no suggestions, describe the following to him. It is called filtering. If you feel inadequate in describing filtering to him, have him read pages 158–161 of this book. *Do not do the filtering until you find an eye doctor who approves,* since for some few children it might be contraindicated by the visual examination. When your eye doctor agrees, begin the following.

Go to your local stationery store and ask for red cellophane which is used for fancy gift wrapping. It usually comes in rolls. Before buying, look through it. You should see a rosy-colored world when looking through it with both eyes. Now look at something which is of the same red color or a pale red color. First look at it with your naked eye and then through the red cellophane. When you look at it through the red cellophane, you will notice that the cellophane acts as a filter and makes the red object change color or disappear.

Now cover only one eye with the red cellophane and look at someone wearing red lipstick. With the uncovered eye you will see the lipstick but, with the covered eye, the lipstick disappears. You can check this by alternately blinking each eye. Red objects disappear when observed through a red filter. When only one eye looks through a filter, you can still see the red object with the other unfiltered eye—but you think you are seeing it with both eyes. Since only one eye can really see the red object, the information is going primarily to one area of the brain for storage.

We can use the same principle with writing. If one of your eyes is covered with a red filter, *it cannot read any writing which is done in a matching red color.* Therefore, only the uncovered eye takes in the word, and the word is sent to a specific storage portion of the brain.

The important thing is to obtain red lead which matches the red of the filter so that the writing completely disappears when observed through the filter. Test a number of red marking pencils and mechanical pencils with red lead. Write with them and then, using both eyes, look at the writing through the filter. The writing that disappears completely when viewed through the filter is the perfectly matched color. If the writing does not disappear when you look at it, then the lead is the wrong color. Keep experimenting until you have the correct shade of red. If you can't find the proper shade of red lead try some orange colors. The proper shade of red or orange will disappear completely when you look at it through the cellophane. Try to find this shade in lead for use in a mechanical pencil.

Ball-point pens will not do because the impressions they make on the surface of the paper are visible, even though the color is invisible.

Next buy a pair of inexpensive sunglasses with frames. Remove both lenses and retain only the frames. Cut a piece of the red cellophane to fit the frame on the side *opposite* your child's handedness. If he is *right-handed*, tape the red cellophane on the frame in front of the *left* eye. If he is *left-handed*, tape the cellophane over the frame in front of the *right eye*. Try the sunglasses on yourself. Through the unfiltered eye everything is seen normally, and through the filtered eye everything has a red hue.

Now, while wearing the glasses, write with the red lead in your mechanical pencil. You will note that you can see your writing very easily.

Now close one eye at a time. The writing, and everything around you, is easily seen with the unfiltered eye. With the filtered eye you can see everything around you, *but not the writing—it disappears!*

We now have a situation where, although both eyes are *seeing*, only one eye is *reading* the red writing. Whenever you write with the red pencil and wear the red filter over one eye, you begin to set up a specific circuiting for writing, while allowing both eyes to see everything else normally. You are now placing the electro-chemical energy in the correct area of the brain.

Now give your child the glasses and the red pencil and ask him to write something. If he normally wears glasses, place the filter on his glasses. Show him how the unfiltered eye is seeing the writing and everything else in the room, while the filtered eye sees everything in the room *except the red writing*. Children are always intrigued by the fact that the writing disappears.

Always use ruled paper with lines a color other than red when you use the red filter. The other-colored lines on ruled paper *do not disappear*. Your child is, therefore, seeing with both eyes.

The unfiltered eye sees the red writing and the lines on the paper. The filtered eye *cannot see the red writing but sees the lines* on the paper. Remember, only the red disappears.

Both eyes are seeing and pouring information into the brain. The filtered eye can't see the words but *can* see the lines. The unfiltered eye is the only eye which can take in the words and the messages are sent to the proper hemisphere of the brain for storage and subsequent retrieval.

You can now begin to have your child use the filter for ten-minute periods of writing. Remember, always use lined paper. You will notice that your child's writing quickly becomes more consistent and more legible. As he adjusts to the filter, he can begin to do some of his homework using the red pencil and the filter.

If he has no homework, have him write a story for practice. If he is in first or second grade, have him copy from a book or copy a story which you have written for him.

Children of seven and eight should have no more than two ten-minute periods per day of filtering; children of nine and ten should have no more than three ten-minute periods per day, and children of eleven and above should not have more than forty-five minutes in 10-to-15-minute periods per day of filtering.

At this time also reinstitute practice with winking, sighting, target sighting, and peephole practice, following the directions on pages 143–144.

After your child has been following these dominant eye activities for *six weeks, test his reading.* If his reading is improving stop the entire program. If not, retest him on eyedness. See tests on pages 117–121. If he is not completely one-sided for eyedness at this time, continue the winking, sighting, target sighting, peep-hole practice, filtering, and add the following:

Take a piece of stiff cardboard and cut a hole exactly one inch wide and six inches long in the right half, if your child is right-sided—or in the left half, if your child is left-sided. See picture below.

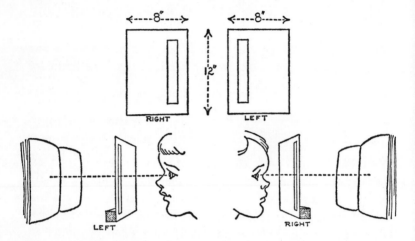

Attach the cardboard to a small wooden block with thumb tacks so that the card will stand up straight; the weight of the wooden block will hold it up straight.

Place the slotted card attached to the wooden block on your child's desk, *three to five inches from his face*. Have him hold his book behind the slotted card. Have him hold the book up straight so that he must look through the hole which you have made in the card to be able to see the book. He may hold the book at any comfortable distance beyond the card. This will usually vary from eight to twelve inches. When properly placed, your child will see the book with one eye only; the other eye being blocked out by the cardboard. While both eyes are seeing, only one is reading. Before having your child read through it, you try it.

As your child starts a reading or homework session, have him do the *first five minutes* looking through the slotted cardboard. This five-minute practice period, using the proper eye-brain channels, stimulates the brain to continue to do so. At the end of the five-minute period, *remove* the slotted cardboard and have your child continue with his reading or his homework.

There may be a tendency on the part of some parents to want to rush the process by just covering one eye while the child reads or writes. We have experimented with covering the sub-dominant eye and we found that this interferes with the two-eyed function of the child. His ability to see in depth is affected. *We do not recommend the covering of an eye.* Remember, both eyes must be seeing, even though only one eye will be reading, during the training periods.

If your child has required this second session of eyedness training in order to establish a dominant eye, stop it at the end of six weeks. He will now have had a total of twelve weeks of eyedness training. At this time stop the entire therapy program, continuing only the supervised study periods or the supervised reading periods. Continue the supervised study and reading periods without eyedness training for a month. *If your child continues to improve in reading, if his performance at school continues to improve and if his eyedness remains consistent with his handedness during this period, stop the entire program.*

Chapter 17

BACK TO NORMAL

YOU HAVE EVALUATED the development of your child's nervous system and you have returned to those stages which he had not completely developed and you have given him the opportunity to develop them. This development for Stages 1, 2, and 3 usually takes from two to four months. The final stage of complete one-sidedness usually takes from two to five months. These times vary according to the amount of additional development which is needed.

When you have completed the program, follow these suggestions.

1. Remember that things we don't do well are frightening or uninteresting to us. Don't pressure your child. Stay with him when he does his homework or reading until he is at ease with them. Praise him for work well done.
2. Never place these developmental activities in conflict with other more attractive activities, such as play or T.V.
3. If he begins to tire while reading, read some of the story *to* him, with him following along on the page.
4. If he doesn't know a word, tell it to him. Don't make him figure it out. There is time enough to teach him how to do this when he is more comfortable with reading.
5. Watch for changes in the type of error he makes, such as reversing words (was to saw) or always missing the same

small words (then, there, where, when). As you see changes, you know that he is making progress.

6. Watch his writing. The goal in writing is to have the vertical slant of all the letters be consistent. Periodically, take a sheet of writing and analyze it by drawing lines from top to bottom at a 45 degree angle, as shown. Then compare the angle of the letters with the pencil lines you made.

7. As you need new books, test them again by having your child read them. If he misses more than two out of ten words, the book is too hard.

8. As the procurement of reading materials becomes a problem, you might visit the book section of one of the large department stores. Many of the stores sell reading workbooks. Choose the workbooks by the same formula: if he misses more than two out of ten words, it is too difficult. If, in your choosing of books for your child, you are unsure of the difficulty level of the books, tend to choose the *easier-to-read book*. It is much better for him if the reading is *too easy* rather than *too hard*.

9. On occasion, tell him what he is going to read about. This helps him to be attuned to what he should learn from the reading.

10. Be sure to point out the progress which your child is making at every opportunity. Success, when recognized, creates greater success.

The question sometimes arises: "I know he can read better, but does he understand what he reads?" This can easily be ascertained by asking questions about what he has read. Ask him to tell you in his own words what he has read.

A natural question is: "How will I know when he is reading well enough?" There are two important measures of this and both of them are required. The first is the report of his reading teacher. It is wise to keep her informed of what you are doing at home and to have periodic chats with her about your child's progress. Her evaluation of his progress is very important. The other, and equally important, measure is simply applied. When your child chooses to read for his own pleasure books which *he* chooses, he is making extremely good progress. Children who read on their own for pleasure teach themselves much more about reading than any reading teacher can. The child who chooses a book, finds a comfortable chair in the living room, and reads of his own volition and with obvious pleasure, is a child who no longer has a reading problem.

You can now allow him to listen to more music; increase it gradually until he is back to a normal amount.

Spelling is the last thing to improve. You will notice that your child will be able to learn to spell on his own *only* after he reads at least at the third-grade level. As his reading improves beyond this level, spelling will begin to improve.

Your job is to provide materials. You have already provided some. Now show your child how to use your local library. Introduce him to the librarian so that he can go to the library independently. In addition to library books, there are many paper books which your child will want to purchase and read. Be careful of the print size, and don't let him buy books with print too small, until he is reading very comfortably.

Remember, when he reads materials *which he chooses,* with understanding and pleasure, he is on his way to becoming a good reader.

The day your child went off to school was a memorable day. The day you suspected, or you were told, that he had a reading problem was an even more memorable day.

The day that both you and the school agree that he has no reading problem will be the *most* memorable day of your child's education, both for you and for him.

Education today is equated with both social and economic success. Children who can't read are dealt with severely by our school system and by our economic system. There is no peace, no work, no success for the child who can't read well enough. There is a stigma attached to the term "drop out."

Employers want employees who have the proper school background and training. Employers always ask for academic credentials. Teaching a child to read is necessary if he is to get on the right social and economic track today.

But there are even more important considerations. To be free, to be an effective citizen in this day and age, requires reading and reading well. Reading is a civil right. One who can't read well in today's world is in great part disenfranchised as a citizen. Many doors are closed. Such a child is severely disabled—not only in school but in all of life.

Overcoming the reading problem is like opening doors. Without it the doors stay closed. The doors to effectiveness and the doors to enjoyment. The doors to success and the doors to happiness.

If reading were just a school subject it wouldn't be as emotionally toned as it is. But it is a key to all school subjects. It is a key to our very humanity.

Children, of course, see reading as a technique which is required by schools and not much more. They have to be taught that it is much more.

To teach a child to read is to teach him to be human. It unshackles him from the need to experience everything which man has experienced, for through reading he can profit from the experience of all who came before us—both the good and bad experiences. No other living creature can do this.

Your child doesn't know about reading, other than as a school subject. If you are to be completely successful in overcoming his problem he must also know what reading is for. In order to ensure his success—show him.

APPENDIX

CHART 1

This random group of 185 children (134 boys and 51 girls) was on a home program supervised by their parents. A normal reader would be expected to make six months' progress in six months. Seventy children in this group made one or more years of progress in six months, thirty showed no progress or had lower scores after this six-month period. The average progress for the entire group of 185 over the six-month period was 8.3 months—exceeding the progress made by normal readers in six months by 2.3 months.

CHART 2

The comparative *rate* of reading growth before and during treatment with this group of 50 normal students with reading problems can be presented graphically. In this group the line 45° to the horizontal would indicate the path of growth of the average child, assuming that the normative data provided by the manufacturers of the test is correct. The new line formed

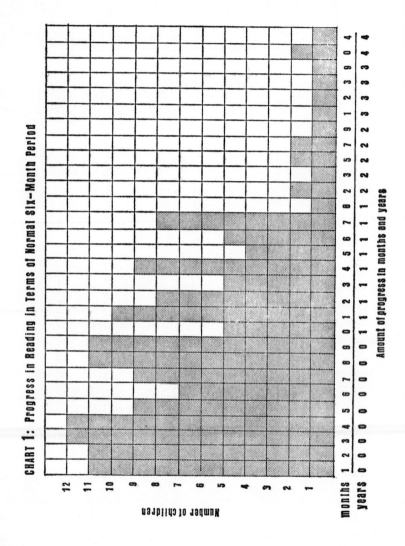

CHART 1: Progress in Reading in Terms of Normal Six-Month Period

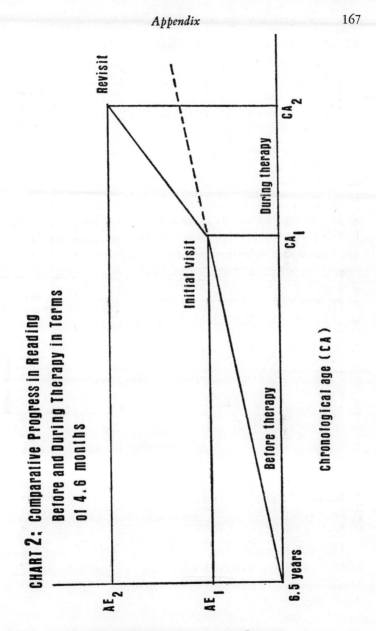

CHART 2: Comparative Progress in Reading Before and During Therapy in Terms of 4.6 months

Reading score in age equivalence (AE)

Chronological age (CA)

at CA_1 forms an Angle (θ), indicating the change of *rate* of progress made by this group of children during the 4.6 months of treatment.*

CASE HISTORY NO. 1

We first saw Randy when he was 11 years and 7 months old and was attending the fifth grade. He was sent to us by his family physician because of his nightly temper tantrums over his English and reading homework and because of his unintelligible spelling. His temper tantrums, both at home and at school, had led to two psychological evaluations. Both psychologists diagnosed Randy as emotionally disturbed. Randy had been taking tranquilizers for a year prior to his coming to us for evaluation.

The history revealed that Randy had been born two weeks prematurely. His development progressed as follows:

4 months—turned over.

6 months—crawled around the dining room.

9 months—pulled himself up to a standing position holding on to furniture.

11 months—walked alone, no longer chose to creep. "A difficult child, happy one minute, miserable the next," the mother reported.

14 months—although Randy had never said words, he started to talk in 3- and 4-word sentences.

Ages 3-4-5—very active but poorly coordinated, hard to discipline.

Ages 6-7-8—attended grades 1, 2, and 3. He had great difficulty, although he seemed bright. Sent to a psychologist because of his behavior and lack of success in school. Temper tantrums increasing.

* Taylor, R., and Nolde, S., "Correlative Study Between Reading Laterality Mobility and Binocularity," *Exceptional Children* (April, 1969), p. 627.

Age 9—repeated 3rd grade. Tutored daily in reading.
Age 10—fourth grade seemed to improve slightly.
Age 11—fifth grade. Tutored during first half of year.
Randy's I.Q. ranged from 110 to 120 on various I.Q. tests.

Evaluation

When we first saw Randy he was reading at a 5.0 grade level. He failed our tests of sleep pattern, creeping, walking, and visual pursuits at all stages. He was right-handed, mixed-footed, and mixed-eyed and his head-paper position was poor. We placed him on a program of sleep pattern, cross-pattern creeping, visual pursuits, walking, and hearing practice.

Second visit:

On this visit his coordination had improved significantly but his creeping and walking were still not perfect. Although his school marks had improved, his reading had only improved slightly—three months. We continued creeping, walking, and visual pursuits in order to make them perfect. We started a sidedness program through right-footedness activities, right-handed activities, filtered writing practice, and deletion of music from his environment.

Third visit:

Randy tested extremely well in coordination and he was becoming right-eyed. His reading score was at the 6.5 grade level, representing an improvement of 1.2 school years. His mother was quite delighted with his behavior and school marks. He hadn't had a temper tantrum for eight weeks. We continued the sidedness program, assigning only a few minutes each day of additional creeping.

Fourth visit:

Randy's coordination was excellent and his sidedness was almost complete. He no longer took tranquilizers and his behavior was completely acceptable. His school marks were excellent. His reading score was 6.3—down two months from his last visit. Because of this we decided to continue the eyedness program for another eight weeks until summer vacation. There would be no program during summer vacation, other than reading for pleasure. Randy was to report back for retesting after the summer vacation.

Fifth visit:

Randy tested well in all developmental areas and he was completely right-sided. His grade level reading score at this time was 7.6. This represented a 2½ year growth over the scores which he made on his first visit. His temper tantrums no longer existed. He was discharged.

CASE HISTORY NO. 2

Patient's Birth Date   August 15, 1958

Reason for Referral Experiencing reading difficulties in school

Grade Placement (school)

| First Visit | 2.2 |
| Last Visit | 4.5 |

Reading Level (Standardized Tests)

| First Visit | 2.1 |
| Last Visit | 5.1 |

Developmental

Never crawled. Did very little creeping and that was done at 19 months of age. Walked at 19½ months. Was hyperactive. When able to run, ran all the time and with abnormal number of falls.

School Reports

Having a difficult time with phonics and arithmetic. Reversals were evidenced, as were omission of words and letters when reading. Child was working in a first-grade reading book.

Short attention span, over-active, and easily distractible were the complaints registered by the school.

D. did most of the developmental tasks reasonably well but he did none of them perfectly. He was right-handed but used his left unconsciously for many activities.

It took one full year of program at home to perfect his crawling, creeping, walking, and to perfect his two-sided activity.

Following this difficult portion of the program a full right-sided program was initiated, and D. finally began to make progress in reading. As his reading improved, his school performance began to improve. He was on a program for 2.3 years, during which time he made 3.0 years reading progress. His reading had improved so that one month before discharge his report card consisted of all A's and B's. Although this had been a very long and difficult program, D. assured us upon his discharge that he was delighted that he could now compete with his classmates.

CASE HISTORY NO. 3

Patient's birth date   April 23, 1958

Reason for referral   Reading and verbal expression problem

Reading Level

    First Visit   2.0

    Last Visit   3.8

Time on Program   9 months

Reading Growth   1 year, 8 months

Developmental

Patient did no creeping in first year of life, but at age 10 months he walked. Started to talk about 2½ years of age and had stammering problems up to date of initial evaluation. Hyperactivity was noted early and continued to be a problem at onset of program. H. had difficulty getting to sleep because of the hyperactivity.

School Reports

Because of reading difficulties, H. repeated first grade and did so poorly in reading during the repeated year that he spent the entire summer being tutored with stress on phonics. He entered second grade and held his own until mid-year when the school recommended more tutoring. This he received five times per week, one hour per session for five months prior to his initial visit.

The child had been given a complete psychological workup. Findings were: above average intelligence, but was a worrywart who was immature; not characterized as a disturbed child; tutoring in reading was the recommended therapy.

Views at the private school in which he was enrolled were that H. should not continue in this school as he could not meet the demands of a high-pressure environment.

Upon evaluation, we found H. to crawl and creep poorly, visual pursuits poor, and auditory ability inadequate. He had not developed *complete* right-sidedness, although he did most things right-handed.

He carried out a prescribed program at home and on his fourth revisit (9 months of home treatment) he made a reading score of 3.8. Prior to the program he had spent three years in school, had spent one full summer receiving remedial reading, and for 5 months during the second grade had received remedial reading 5 days per week. When first seen he made a grade level score of 2.0, his score 9 months later was 3.8.

H. is now competing successfully at school. He is in a regular group doing "B" work. He now reads for pleasure.